LED BY GOD

The Blessed Journey of a Minister's Wife

By June Temme

LED BY GOD:
The Blessed Journey of a Ministers Wife
By June Temme

ISBN: 978-1-7329400-3-1

Edited by Lil Barcaski and Eli Gonzalez
Book Design by GFAD Designs

Printed in USA

A Note from June

This is my story as I remember it. With the help and encouragement of my husband, family, and friends, it is the story of my life as a minister's wife. It has been a great life, and this book, my labor of love, is my legacy for my children, grandchildren, and great-grandchildren.

I have written this book for your enjoyment. I wrote it, not in my prime, but in my 80s. Raised in a Christian home, I attended Christian schools, married a Christian minister and worshipped in Christian churches around the world; what could have been better!?

I guess God saw more in me than I saw in myself as He has led me all the way through trials and blessings. I have been married to a wonderful man for nearly 63 years. We have three children, ten grandchildren and, at this writing, five great-grandchildren.

Blessings to all who read this book.

Table of Contents

Led by God

Foreword – Rev. David Paech

David has known me for most of my life as we grew up and lived in the same town (Tarrington), Victoria, Australia. We still keep in touch to this day. - June

Dear June,

When we go back 70 or 80 years, some things from that era stick in our minds. Life at Tarrington in the Western Districts of Victoria, Australia, was great! I was the youngest of the local pastor's family. Our large, comfortable manse in a largely Lutheran rural area was next to the "old church," built about 1868. It burnt down before our eyes on January 14, 1944 in a devastating fire that wiped out many homes. Our home was alight in the roof, and my father and older brother fought a losing battle against the flames. However, a roving truck with a water pump saved the manse.

Much worse off were the Ben Noske's, about two miles from the church. Good friends of ours, they lost all their farm buildings. Their family, with daughters Eleanor and June, were good friends and we had some great meals at their very hospitable home. Ben and Viola, their parents, were very friendly and forward-looking farmers, and I liked going to their farm. We rode bikes and climbed in quarries midway between our homes. Being the last of a family of five, I found friends in the girls, and they seemed to feel the same about me.

After about 25 years in the Tarrington parish, my Dad accepted a call to take charge of migrant workers in Victoria and Tasmania, and we moved to Melbourne. However, as a new pastor, in my second parish, we were only about 30 miles from the Temmes where June's husband Hu was the first Lutheran pastor in the new city called Elizabeth. They had moved from an Aboriginal mission hundreds of miles away.

It was on the way from our home to Adelaide, so we often visited. We played golf, and the two young families were about the same age.

Now it has been occasional emails! Writing this brings back many memories. I wish them well in their retirement. We are in the same circumstances and much the same age.

Rev. David Paech. Adelaide, South Australia

Foreword –Val Dutschke

Val and I both went to Concordia College, Adelaide in 1950. After our marriages, Hubert and I went to Yalata as missionaries. Val and Erwin were the Colona Station Managers and we met again in Elizabeth, South Australia. - June

I am so pleased, June, that you asked me to write a few words for your exciting record of your busy life since we were students at Concordia College, Adelaide, South Australia. I thought you were such a good athlete and a great basketball player.

Fancy both of us met again as wives of staff workers at the Yalata Aboriginal Mission. Remember those days when the temperature was over 100 degrees and we had no air conditioning in our homes? And each morning at our door there was a small group of nomad natives wanting some food, or clothing sent to us by kind ladies in Lutheran congregations around the State of South Australia.

Sometimes the request was for medicine for a serious illness. Then my husband, Erwin, flew the patient to the nearest hospital. Quite often, travelers broke down in their cars on the long dirt road across Australia and needed help. Lucky for them my husband was also a mechanic.

But they were great times – little did we know when we were at college together we would end up as missionaries helping each other as staff members, and so many needy people.

Erwin and I appreciated your open home where we often had a Sunday lunch after church – or a relaxing game of cards. We had such a great friendship that when we retired from our position as Station Managers, we became members of your congregation in Elizabeth, near Adelaide – and we remained close friends even when you moved to the USA.

Love you, June, and thanks for recording the exciting work to which God led you.

Val Dutschke, Elizabeth, South Australia.

EXTRAORDINARY WOMAN! EXTRAORDINARY LIFE!

June Noske Temme is that person. June has been my dear and treasured friend since Oct. 1991 when she moved to Hong Kong. She came with her husband Hu who was the new pastor of the Church of All Nations, a Lutheran Church connected to Hong Kong International School (HKIS) on Hong Kong Island. Our children attended HKIS and our family were members of the Church. We welcomed this vibrant, full of life, dynamic native Australian couple with these amazing Aussie accents into that community. June and Hu quickly became close personal friends and have remained so long after leaving Hong Kong and until this day. During our times together, June would recall stories of times during her life's journey which were riveting, inspiring and fascinating! After hearing these stories we would always respond "June, you need to write a book!" After all these years she called me to say that she was taking our challenge and writing a book about her life. YES!!! That she asked me to write the foreword to her book is an honor and a privilege.

JUNE IS AN EXTRAORDINARY WOMAN

Strong faith in God

Loving wife, mother, grandmother, great grandmother
Loyal friend

Fearless regardless of age

Seeker of adventure and travel

Fit and athletic (played tennis well into her 70's and still plays nine holes of golf weekly at 84)

JUNE HAS AN EXTRAORDINARY LIFE

Survived a terrible fire as a child in Australia

Left Sydney, Australia in May 1968 with Hu and 3 young children on a ship via Hong Kong, Japan, Hawaii, Los Angeles reaching their final destination, Centralia, Illinois in July 1968

Survivor of back surgery and skin cancer

World traveler

Ageless

Can-do spirit

My favorite story is in 2008 when June and Hu traveled to visit us when we lived in Edinburgh, Scotland. Not only did they get the full experience of Edinburgh including watching the world-famous Edinburgh Military Tattoo in the pouring rain getting soaked to the bone, but they also rented a car and had a detailed road trip planned throughout Scotland over mountains, less traveled highways and byways with Hu driving and June navigating. They invited us to come along... which we did! WHAT A TRIP!! Driving on the opposite side of the road takes a bit of getting used to, but they were pros. We were chauffeured all over Scotland staying in small inns and dining in small, local restaurants. Their visit is without question one of the highlights and favorite memories of our two years in Scotland.

June is one of my "Sheroes." I can't wait to read her book, relive the stories she shared with us and learn more about my EXTRAORDINARY FRIEND.

With love and gratitude,

Anita Rhodes Shrigley, Lafayette, CA

Oct. 2018

***

When I think of June, I'm reminded of Priscilla in the New Testament. She and her husband Aquila were dependable partners to each other and to the apostle Paul in his mission for the Lord Jesus. June and Hubert are like that. I first met them in 1974 when I was a freshly-minted pastor in southern Illinois. The congregation they served was the largest and among the most vibrant in our circuit of congregations. I learned from them. Years later, I again had the privilege of seeing June in working partnership with her husband. Hu was a gift officer for Concordia Seminary. He would arrange events where I could meet donors and talk about the Lord's mission through the Seminary. It was June who most carefully attended to all the details, checking arrangements time and again, serving as a most gracious host and with a positive attitude and smile I'll always treasure; June showed her love for her Lord and His Church, just like Priscilla. Enjoy the stories she tells. June Temme has much to teach us about life and service under our Lord Jesus.

Rev. Dr. Dale A. Meyer, President

Concordia Seminary, St. Louis, Missouri

Prologue

Family History

Growing up in Tarrington, Victoria, Australia

My Church

My father always claimed that he could trace our ancestry back to Charlemagne the Great. Remember him from your history lessons? He was born in 742 AD, and in Rome, Pope Leo the third crowned him emperor of the Roman Empire. He was a fine Christian man.

Can you imagine the fun we siblings had at our family gatherings as we made up stories about our famous forefather? Sometimes, our imaginations went too far, but of one thing we are certain: my great-great-great-grandfather Pastor Clamor Schurmann came from Prussia in Europe to be a Missionary to the Aborigines in Port Lincoln, South Australia.

The year was 1853, when Pastor Clamor Schurmann was called to Tarrington, Victoria, to become the first Minister to a small settlement of Lutherans in Southern Victoria. He started St. Michael's Lutheran Church and, in its 150 years of history, three church buildings were erected. The last one is a very large Gothic brick church holding over 700 people. When it was built in 1928, my father was president of the Luther League (Walther League). The youth group decided to donate the baptismal font. They had a large marble angel carved in Italy and shipped to Tarrington. When it arrived at the church, it was too heavy for the floorboards. To support it, a slab of concrete was placed underneath the flooring. My paternal grandfather Noske built and carved the very large ornate hymn boards still used to this day. I was baptized, confirmed and married in St. Michael's.

My Grandparents

Herman Noske married Emilie Louise Mibus on 24th January 1889. In my father's family there were nine children. Three died in infancy and my father, Bernhard Edmund (Ben), was the youngest.

My grandmother's sister went to live with my grandparents when her husband died. Shortly thereafter, she fell ill with tuberculosis and died. Later, when my Dad was just four years old, Emilie (Dad's mother) died from the same disease, which was not treatable in those days. She had contracted it from her sister. My grandfather was left a widow with six children whose ages ranged from 4 to 16 years. He remarried and he and his new wife had a boy and two girls. Unfortunately, grandfather died when he was just 24 years old, leaving behind a wife and young children.

Herman Noske was a farmer and was very skilled in cabinet-making, which was a hobby for him. He made a hand-operated Merry-Go-Round for the annual school picnics which were held on his farm very close to the church and school yard. He made the stone cross with ornamental stonework on the gables of the blue stone church.

My father's one sister, Alma, never married, but had a career in midwifery nursing. She trained at the Queen Victoria Hospital, Melbourne, Victoria, and then, in 1938, went to London to finish her studies as an Infant Welfare sister. She was privileged to meet the Queen (the Queen Mother) when she visited the hospital where Aunty Alma was training. The Queen asked to see the new nurses who had come from around the commonwealth. As WWII had just started, the nurses were sent home and she returned to Australia on the Queen Mary. It was the last voyage before the ship was stripped and turned into a troop and transport ship for the soldiers going overseas to fight in the war. She returned to Horsham, Victoria where she was in charge of the Baby Health Center until her untimely death in a car accident in 1957 at age 64 years. She was my sponsor at my Christening and I admired her very much.

My father (Ben) took over his brother's farm when Ern moved north after he was married. The farm was adjacent to the family farm. We saw his older brother, Uncle Alf, quite a lot as he purchased a farm about 20 miles from Tarrington. The other members of the family lived much further away so we didn't see as much of them. Some died early in life.

My Mother's Parents

My mother's father was Johannes (John or Jack) Habel and was married to Bertha Schurmann in 1904. They lived in a large house built of blue stone from a quarry on the property at Yulecart, west of Hamilton.

My mother Viola (Vi) had two sisters and three brothers.

Mum's father became well-known in the district as the first to breed stud sheep and cattle. He won numerous prizes for his sheep and wool throughout Australia. On several occasions he gained first prize for his wool fleeces at the Royal Show in London. His many ribbons and medals were the pride of his family. I was lucky enough to acquire one of the prize ribbons.

My mother had a lovely singing voice and with her musical siblings, who played the piano, guitar, banjo, mandolin or violin, entertained us when we visited.

At Christmas time we would go to the homestead for a lovely Christmas dinner. We gathered in the very large living room when Father Christmas made an appearance to hand out presents. I was a little scared and snuggled up to my mother when he came near me.

Many years later my grandparents Bertha and Jack Habel moved into the larger town of Hamilton where they built a much smaller home, but still with a very large dining room to accommodate the large family for special occasions. As it was customary in those days, my mother's brothers inherited the farm. The girls had to give up their rights and sell their portion to the boys. Very unfair, but that is how it was for their inheritance. Hamilton was a larger town 5 miles from Tarrington where I grew up. When my mother went into town to shop she always took some homemade butter, eggs, and veggies to my grandmother. My grandmother was a great flower gardener and took fresh cut flowers regularly to the hotels and businesses in town. She didn't drive so she walked the two miles carrying large bunches of flowers.

Living next door to them in Hamilton was a man called Reginald (Reg) Ansett who started a bus industry in Hamilton going out to all corners of the Western District of Victoria. He also started a plane service to Melbourne and other parts of Victoria. Ansett Airlines later grew to be one of the major airlines in Australia.

We loved visiting my mother's sister, Ruby Bunge, as they had electricity and could make homemade ice cream. She always had some in the freezer when we visited them.

My Parents - Ben & Viola (Vi) Noske

My parents, Bernhard Edmund (Ben) Noske and Viola (Vi) Habel were married in the Tarrington Lutheran Church on 15th April 1931.

They spent their honeymoon at Appolo Bay and Lorne on the Great Ocean Road. It is one of the world's most famous coastal drives, 150 miles along the south west coast of Victoria. It's famous for the twelve apostles, large craggy limestone rocks towering above the ocean. They played croquet on the lawn in front of the hotel with kangaroos occasionally jumping around.

My Dad owned a motorbike when he was courting my mother, riding to her home in Yulecart fifteen miles from his farm. After they were married he bought a car for more comfort for my mother.

Dad played in the Tarrington Brass Band for many years. For special church services they entertained the members by playing hymns outside the church. He was active in the congregation by serving as a trustee and secretary.

My father was a member of the Australian Light Horse Brigade (cavalry), and was chosen with his horse to be an escort for the Duke and Duchess of York when they visited Melbourne. This royal couple later became King George VI and Queen Elizabeth (the Queen Mother) of the British Commonwealth.

I grew up with an older sister Eleanor, and twelve years later my mother had another daughter Lynette, then three years after that, another daughter Elizabeth. It was not so good living and working on a farm with no boys, but we did our best to be of use to Dad.

Part One

Childhood, War, and Marriage

June Temme

Chapter 1

Farm Life

"Alright, now June, you will be the Preacher and I will be the woman in the congregation with the baby. Just stand there on the veranda and lead us in prayer and song."

I was five years old and my sister Eleanor was two years my senior, she didn't play with me very much. But when she did, she loved to play "Church." I was always the Preacher and she the long-suffering mother whose baby would surely cry during my sermon causing her to rise and excuse herself, exiting the imaginary church with the imaginary screaming child.

"Oh, no! Baby is crying again. I have to take her outside to calm her. Continue preaching," she would say and so I did. When she returned a few minutes later, we would sing all our favorite hymns. I could never imagine how this game would turn out to be a foreshadowing of my future.

Nor could I have known how much our idyllic life would change. The winds of war were blowing but at five years of age that meant little to me. I couldn't fully grasp what was coming or how it would forever change not only my world but everyone else's.

For me and my family, life was simple and lovely. We lived and worked on our farm in the Western Districts of Victoria in Southern Australia. My father bred sheep; not just any sheep, fine Merino sheep, which produced the highest-quality wool.

In 1939 I was five years old. My life consisted of chores, play, church, and school. When I wasn't doing chores or schoolwork I would often play with my many dolls and the little doll pram I used to take for walks. I loved the little playroom my father had made for us next to the workers room and near our garden. When I tired of being indoors, I would load all my dolls into the pram and take them for a walk along the ruts in the road made by the machinery tracks. I had a big stuffed bear, which was ironically made in Germany. He was a rather big bear, filled with straw, and I never went anywhere without him. His fur would often wear off and my mother would patch him up and make sure his stuffing was secure. My bear, dolls and I would sit under the Sheoak tree on a big branch and I would tell them elaborate stories I made up out of my wild imagination. In my heart, I believe they listened and loved every word.

Word of the War Comes to Us

Since Australia was under the rule of the British empire, if England went to war, Australia would also be at war. Winston Churchill was the British Prime Minister and he was a beloved figure. My Dad loved him as much as any man. Churchill was a Navy man who knew the strengths required for great leadership. While, at five, I couldn't understand politics, I knew that when Churchill's voice came over the airways and into our living room via the big family radio, everyone was rapt with attention listening to his positive messages.

My father came from getting supplies in town. He had a newspaper under his arm.

"We're at war." father spoke softly to mother but I overheard his worried words. "We must be prepared." "Oh, no! Our poor boys," mother replied.

For my sister and me it didn't register at first what being at war meant. Even with my strong imagination, the most I could envision was our local boys being hurt or killed. I had no deep understanding and I didn't think life would change much.

But it did.

Very quickly we saw the local boys disappearing, heading off for basic training to prepare to do their part. Soon there was no one to help at the farm. Their leaving created a big hole in the population of our little community. After a short while they began returning to town in their crisp new uniforms, home on leave before deployment. We would see them in church looking far more grown up than they were just a few weeks ago. Everyone would tell them how proud we were of them. In church, school, and at home we prayed for their safe return.

Work Around the Farm

With the local boys gone our chores increased. But we never resented chores. Our parents helped us to make them fun. We didn't know anything else. Working on a farm meant pitching in doing what needed to be done. It was simply a matter of fact.

Mum would take us out to help with the crops. We grew oats and had to harvest the chaff for the horses. We had six work horses, a riding horse, and one horse to pull our little Jinka; a small wagon in which I loved to ride. It was always a treat when father would let me ride in it on the back roads.

We also grew meadow hay for the sheep. The horses pulled the machines that mowed grass and baled it into stacks. Our draft horses were very strong and could easily pull the machinery. The oats were cut and a machine bundled them into sheaves. Mother would take us out and we stood the bundles up into pyramid like structures called stooks. Dad would come with the horses and wagon along with a neighbor who would help us as that there were no young men to hire. Dad stood on top of the wagon and stacked the sheaves as the neighbor tossed them to him. Then he would build a haystack. We put the hay through a chaff cutter so it would be ready for the horses to eat. On one occasion I was walking behind the wagon when the horses were spooked by a rabbit and bolted. After much yelling and pulling on the reins, the horses finally calmed down and Dad continued with the loading of hay on the wagon.

I was only five or six when I climbed up on a hay stack and fell down and broke my arm. My sister and I had been sliding down the stacks, giggling wildly, our faces flush with the excitement of the game. I slid down and clamored back several times but then I had a misstep. As I slid, I twisted and landed on my arm and heard a snap even before I realized the pain shooting through my arm.

"Mother! Help," I cried out.

She came running, scooping me up and carrying me to the farmhouse. They took me to the doctor's office and fixed me up. It mended quickly after being set in a cast, which I wore like a badge of honor.

Another time, my sister, Eleanor got too close to a horse in the stable. The horse was jittery and all of a sudden reared up and kicked her in the head. Luckily, she was not seriously hurt other than her pride. Lesson learned.

The only hospital in Hamilton, where I was born, was called "Kia Ora" which in New Zealand Maori means "good health." I think other than major illnesses or catastrophes most of the farmer's families never went to the hospital. Maybe the name was a good omen for keeping us safe and in "good health."

Things happen on a farm. You learn to brush things off and go on. You learn to be tough and strong. I had no idea as a child, how much these experiences were preparing me for a most interesting and vivid life as a Minster's wife.

We never minded the work around the farm. One of my earliest memories is of father teaching me to whistle while walking behind him while he was directing his horses pulling a plough. Somehow the whistling made the time go faster and the work seemed more like play.

We fed the chickens and gathered the eggs. I milked the cow in the morning before school and in the evening and then I would run the separator to separate the milk from the cream. I used a hand-operated butter churn to make butter, and then my mother would make several pounds of butter. Homemade butter was always much tastier that store bought.

My father gave me some leftover seeds from his vegetable planting. I had my own vegetable and flower garden near the orchard. I was very happy when, for the evening meal, my mother would cook the vegetables I had grown for us to eat. It made me quite proud to watch my family enjoy the fruits of my labor, or to be more precise, the vegetables of my labor.

I loved to pick fruit from our orchard; cherries, apples, pears, plums, prunes, peaches, nectarines, mulberries, and figs. Sometimes I ate so much fruit I wasn't hungry for the evening meal. We even had a grape arbor.

On wash days I would help my mother peg the clothes on the large square line outside the garden fence but still in the large area enclosed with trees on four sides. We would have to watch for rain mostly in the winter. My Dad was very good at predicting rain. He watched the clouds with great insight and sometimes we had to rush out and bring all the wet wash inside and then hang it out all over again. Later we had a rotary clothes line installed in the garden area.

Dad had a shed where grain was stored when there was very little grass in the paddocks for the sheep. Eleanor and I would play in there because there was an old trunk filled with fun things. Dad's old army uniform with his plumed ostrich hat was fun to wear, or we would look at old pictures. We would try to blow into his brass instrument from when he played in the Tarrington brass band, but we could never get much of a sound from it. His violin was there as well. Sometimes we would see a mouse eating the grain and running around the bags of oats. That would scare us.

As a child I remember sitting on a box with holes in it near the old machinery shed. I watched what I thought were flies going in and out. Turned out to be bees, but lucky as I was, I did not get stung.

The sheep shearing shed was about four feet off the ground. The sheep poop would fall through the gratings onto the ground below. One of our jobs was to scoop up the poop and load it into a wheelbarrow to be spread around the garden beds. Sheep manure was a great fertilizer for flowers and vegetables.

Out in the paddocks where the cows grazed we picked wild mushrooms. Cow manure made for great mushrooms.

We had two extinct volcanoes in the area and sometimes we would have a picnic and climb to the top for a wonderful view of the surrounding landscape.

And of Course, There Were the Sheep

Shearing time was once a year in the spring and we would start by helping round up the sheep. My father trained his own sheep dogs (Border Collies) to round up the sheep with a whistle. He just used his fingers in his mouth for different instructions. We were never allowed to actually shear the sheep, that was work for a grown man and there was a very special skill to it which is shearing without cutting the sheep's skin. But once in a while Dad would let me hold the shears while he guided my very small hands with his very large ones. It made me feel as though I was part of the process. Most of the shearing was done by the shearers who came around when it was the season. But during the war many of them were off fighting for our country.

Neighbors came to help but it was a skill to hand shear a sheep. Everyone had to pitch in and help at shearing time. My mother would take morning tea and afternoon tea to the shearing shed with pots of tea, and her homemade cakes and biscuits (cookies).

After the sheep were shorn the wool fleeces were placed into very large strong hessian bags about 3 feet square by 6 feet high which were then placed in a wood frame. These were called bales. Dad enlisted our help with the stomping down of the wool, To us, this was a particularly fun chore. Dad lifted us up and dropped us into the bales of wool. It was our job to stomp down the wool with our bare feet as much as we could.

"Step down harder, June. Jump up and down" Dad cried out and I would give it my all. "There you go!" he said proudly.

After we finished with this monumental task, our feet and hands were as soft as could be from the natural lanolin of the soft sheep's wool.

Finally, a heavy press would be placed on top of the wool bales to finish the job.

Our sheep yielded fine Merino wool. These were the only kind of sheep we had. The wool from these sheep was of the highest quality one could find. Both before and after the war, the Japanese still came to the markets to buy this fine wool.

The bales had to be specifically branded with Dad's name and the name of our farm, which was "Glenora." Special black paint was used for this purpose. All farmers were required to do this. "Glenora" is a name we have used to name our homes in which we have lived.

The bales were sent to Geelong about 80 miles away where they would wait for the wool auction. Bidding was quite fierce when exceptional wool was being auctioned to people from many countries including the Japanese who desired my Dad's fine Merino wool.

On one occasion, when I was about eight years old, I accompanied Dad to the wool sales. That year he topped the market. There was much rejoicing. Amazingly, the little guy with one small sheep farm beat out the big farmers!

Basic Needs

We had two large galvanized tanks attached to the house with rainwater from the roof. It was sufficient water for household use so we didn't need the water from the underground tank. There were also two very large tanks on high stands outside the garden fence and those were filled from the dam which was powered by a windmill. That water was used to water the flower and vegetable garden with hose sprinklers. That water was not for household use as the water came from the dam where the sheep would drink.

Dad stood under one of the tanks on the stands when he needed to butcher a sheep. He would choose one of the older male sheep and it was quite a process. No part of the sheep would go to waste. First he pulled out the brains and liver. Sheep brains and liver were quite a favorite. Butchers would sell them. Dad would then leave the rest of the sheep in a bag to keep cool under the tank stand. He dried out the skins as skin buyers wanted to buy them. Mum would sell the skins for her shopping money. Their worth was in the weight of the skin. We kept half the butchered sheep and gave half to a neighbor who would do the same when it was his turn to do the butchering. We had no refrigeration, so keeping more than half would mean a lot of spoiled meat. To keep the meat cool we had a structure called a "Cool Safe" covered in hessian, a bag of thin material that when wet helped keep things cool inside it. Cold water was kept on top that would drip down so that the hessian could soak it up, cooling the structure with the food in it. We had a similar one with a deep hole in the ground under it in the kitchen.

We also had an underground water tank just outside the back verandah. It held very cold water. My Dad would lower a bucket on a rope with a bottle of beer, which was the size of a soda bottle. When he pulled the bottle back up later, the beer was nice and cold to drink. It was a treat for the workers who helped on the farm during harvesting, shearing and other jobs. There was a hand pump attached to get cold water for drinking. We didn't use that water very often.

Once in a while, during lambing season, a mother sheep would die or a lamb was born that needed extra care. When that happened the lamb was brought into the house and kept near the stove in the kitchen for warmth. We fed the little lambs with a bottle. For us this was big fun, and they would become our pets until they were able to be put into the house yard, and then back with the flock.

That same wood-burning stove kept the kitchen warm, but not the bedrooms. In cold weather we would hunker down in our beds under an eiderdown which is a cover filled with feathers from the eider duck. In particularly cold weather we filled hot water bags for our feet and we had woolly bed socks just for sleeping. Then we were always warm and cozy in our beds, unless the water bags broke and then we would have a wet bed--a most unpleasant outcome to be avoided.

As little kids on cold mornings, we got dressed in front of the stove to get ready for school. On Sundays we wore cotton stockings. These were to be worn only for church. We needed suspenders with snaps to clip at the thigh to hold up the stockings.

***

As the war became more and more a reality, we found ourselves at night, sitting in the warmth near the stove, listening to the big wooden radio for news of the fighting. Our radio was so large it was a big piece of furniture and touted the little dog who was listening to "His Master's Voice." Many nights we heard the voice of Prime Minister Churchill and our own leaders giving us words of encouragement. Sometimes we would even hear from the King of England, George the Fifth and, later, George the Sixth.

The radio was run by a large wet battery, something like the batteries that run cars today. We had two batteries so that one could be taken into town to be charged while the other kept us closer to the world outside our peaceful lives.

Soon, the war beyond our shores would come to us.

Chapter 2

The War Comes Closer to Home

The war started in 1939 and I was five years old and had just started school. I remember trying to understand currency. It was one of the first ways we learned arithmetic. Our money was called Pounds, Shillings, and Pence. The pound notes were all different colors depending on the denomination. For example, a one-pound note was green whereas a five-pound was blue, unlike American money which is all one color. In addition, the one-pound note was a bit smaller than the five-pound note, and so on. Twelve pence made up one shilling, ten shillings made a note. Twenty shillings made a pound note but, just to confuse us, 21 shillings was one guinea. Then there were three pence and sixpence coins. My goodness, arithmetic was difficult for us kids.

Once the war started, rationing began almost immediately. Our arithmetic came in handy. Sugar, flour, tea, and petrol, even clothing, required coupons. You needed to save for a year to buy a suit.

My mother, ever the resourceful one, started remaking old material into clothes. On her Singer treadle sewing machine, she made dresses from used material. She knitted our cardigans & jumpers (sweaters). Skeins of wool yarn were much more readily available at first, but eventually, even they were rationed. I learned to knit when I started school at age five. I knitted scarves and later a cardigan for my twelfth birthday. My mother showed me how to darn socks a certain way so toes wouldn't poke through the new darn.

Preparing for Attack

Not only were we learning arithmetic, reading, and writing in school, we were learning what to do in case we were attacked during a school session. There were air raid drills and we would file out of the school house and jump down into the trenches that the local farmers dug for us. They wanted to make sure we were safe if we were attacked. The big tree roots around the school made it tough, but they managed to dig down about three-feet and create zig-zag-shaped ditches that were meant to protect us from gunfire or bombs. I have no idea if they would have actually worked, and luckily we never had to find out, but I can say that we kids loved air raid drills. It was an exciting break from our school work.

The school bell would ring as if we were having a fire drill, and our teacher would quickly rise from her desk. "Children, children. Everyone up from your desks and line up single file. Follow me. We're going to our trenches to practice."

There were just two teachers in our two-room school house, and they taught the fifty or so children entrusted to their education. There was one teacher for grades 1 through 4 and one for grades 5 through 8.

Once outside, we ran to the trenches and jumped in. The trenches were really rather small so most of us could stand about waist deep. The older boys were told to crouch down and frankly most of us were still head and shoulders taller than the depth of the trenches. The whole exercise was good fun for us. We were never really scared.

Our teachers tried to make us feel like it was real. In hindsight, the trenches were so close to school that if the little building had been bombed, we would have probably been in the line of fire of the flying debris. I couldn't really think about what it meant. The war was over there, far away from our quiet little lives, but we did realize that our boys were also over there.

Small Efforts

I knew boys from church and older brothers of school mates who were fighting for us. We continued to say prayers in church and school. Eventually, there would be much rejoicing when they came back, but that would not happen for a while for most of our soldiers and their families.

In school, the boys were taught woodworking and other skills useful around a farm while we learning to sew and knit. We had knitting and sewing classes for the girls taught by one of the local ladies. I made a pair of long pajamas for myself only by hand stitching without a sewing machine. They were nice winter material and very warm.

Also we knitted scarves, socks, and gloves for the soldiers in Army and Navy colors. The wool skeins were provided to us by the Red Cross. We attached our name and address and sometimes we received a thank you note from a military person. It was so exciting to get one of those notes. It made us feel more grown-up and as if we were contributing to the war effort.

War or No War, Celebrations Continued

One tradition we enjoyed was celebrating Guy Fawkes on November 5th. Mr. Fawkes (1570-1606) along with his co-conspirators, planned to blow up both Houses of Parliament in London. He was caught, tortured, and hanged.

On Guy Fawkes Day, we saved all the dry limbs and branches from trees and put them in a very high pile in the house yard. My parents bought very inexpensive fire crackers, like jumping jacks, sky-rockets, and Catherine wheels. We invited neighbors to watch the display and had a great evening when it got dark enough to light the fire. We always had water close by to put out any sparks that might have ignited the grass. Surprisingly, there were no injuries on these nights.

Churches celebrated a Harvest Thanksgiving festival. It was usually held in or around March. Members would gather their finest fruit and vegetables and take them to the church the day before, to decorate the front of the church. Loaves of bread were baked, and together with a glass of water were placed on the altar. Flowers decorated the sanctuary. It was a beautiful display. The minister and teachers could first take whatever they wanted to eat, preserve, make jam, etc. The rest was given to poor people.

Talking about celebrations – now living in America I hear the question. "June, do you have July 4th in

Australia?" This is my answer: "Of course. Every country has a July 4th."

Christmas was a special time for us. We went with Dad to pick out a pine tree to bring to the house for decorations. We only had candles on little holders that we clipped onto the branches as there was no electricity.

Then we went to our room to lie down and rest for the evening service. We didn't know it, but our parents quickly decorated the tree with colored balls, garlands, and holiday fare. After we had our evening meal we went to church to celebrate Christmas Eve.

In school we practiced our memory lines and carols to perform in the church on Christmas Eve. We loved going into the big church for a rehearsal before the big night. We had to speak and sing loudly because there was no amplification. We learned everything by heart. We all wore our best Sunday clothes. A very large pine tree was beautifully decorated in the front corner, and after the service the School Board handed out bags of sweets and chocolates to the children. After our performance we would rush home to see what "Father Christmas" had left for us.

We were made to sit in the car with Mum so that Dad could make sure Father Christmas was gone. While in the house, he lit the candles on the tree, and then he came back to the car and would say, "He is gone so we can go in now." We would enter the dining room to find packages placed carefully under the tree. We were always surprised by what we received.

My Aunty Alma often visited us for Christmas. She always gave us lovely gifts. One year she made beautiful dresses for Eleanor and me to wear to church. We wore them the very next day for the Christmas Day service. Because December in Australia is in the middle of our summer, we were able to show off our dresses because they were unencumbered by an overcoat.

Among the many books Auntie Alma gave me are my favorites, *Milly, Molly, Mandy Stories*; *More of Milly, Molly, Mandy*; and *Further Doings of Milly, Molly, Mandy*. My daughter, Lisa, has been begging me for years to give them to her. She will get her wish one day.

For Christmas dinner, instead of lamb, my mother sometimes cooked a goose which she purchased. A tradition in Australia is a plum pudding for dessert. My mother boiled some silver coins, three pence, six pence, and maybe a shilling or two, to put into the pudding. She made it the day before and put it into a cloth bag to steam the next day in a pot. It was served with wonderful vanilla custard. Beside loving the pudding, we ate ourselves sick to get as many coins as we could because we could keep them.

Easter was another joy and excitement. Before church we received a basket with chocolate Easter eggs and bunnies, but we had to wait until after church before we could eat them. We squirmed a little through the service, knowing what lovely delicacies waited for us. During the war, chocolate was much scarcer, but mother and father did their best to save up to get us some as a treat.

Even during the war years we managed to find joy in our celebrations at home and in our church. Those were happy times as we put the war at bay enjoying our family and friends.

America Enters the War

Two years later, December 7ᵗʰ, 1941, the Japanese bombed Pearl Harbor and America was finally in the war. Pearl Harbor was a very sad event and we all mourned the loss of American life, but we were happy to see England and Australia getting help from the Americans. We were especially happy that they were fighting the Japanese who were too close to us for comfort.

Our parents and our Pastor talked with great joy about the fact that the Americans were in the fight. Even if, at the tender age of 8, I didn't fully understand what it meant, I understood that Americans were our great allies, our friends.

You could feel the hope in the way people spoke and acted. The Americans were going to defend Australia.

In August of 1942, American engaged in the Battle of Guadalcanal. It was the first major offensive and decisive victory for the Allies in the Pacific. The Japanese had troops stationed in that section of the Solomon Islands. Bear in mind that the distance from Australia to the Solomon Islands is only *2,039 miles*. A little too close for comfort for us. The U.S. marines launched a surprise attack and took control of an air base that was under construction. Our own Minister's oldest son was drafted at that time and fought the Japanese alongside the Americans in the Islands of New

Guinea, Bougainville, and Emirau. When he returned, after the war, he brought back many Japanese souvenirs including a Samurai sword which he later presented to the Returned Soldier Museum in Hamilton, Victoria.

The Japanese lost a total of 24,000 men in the Battle of Guadalcanal, while the Americans troops saw 1,600 killed, 4,200 wounded, as well as several thousand dead from malaria and other tropical diseases. It was a game-changer for the war and it meant something else to us personally. American soldiers would be coming to us for Rest and Recuperation (R and R) They were Marines and they typically spent two weeks with us.

The Aussies and the Yanks always got on very well. We were especially grateful to the Americans. When their boys came to visit us in the summer of 1943 to rest up and enjoy a little free time away from the war, they brought silk stockings, cigarettes, chocolate, and Wriggly's chewing gum. Everyone enjoyed having them around. They seemed bigger than life to us kids. Real, live G.I. Joes.

The only time they caused a ruckus was when the American boys would steal the girls away from the Aussie boys. Girls clamored to be around the American Marines. They were exciting and exotic to them with their big attitudes and odd accents, particularly the New Yorkers and the Texans. The Texans bragged about their big cars and 10-gallon hats and the New York boys, well, they came from the most exciting city in the world. It was like they were from a different planet than our little town. And they had money. Going to America meant becoming rich. It wasn't hard for them to steal away a few of the local girls from their beaus.

Regardless, America's involvement in WW II set up a great friendship that still exits. Australians still view visiting America as high on their bucket list and vice versa.

For us kids, the Americans visits to our home were a bit magical. They were so full of life. I remember them teaching us to swim the dog paddle in the dam. They were always nice to us. In reality, most of them were just young boys themselves, hardly much older than we were. Despite the fact that they were marines and were supposed to be worldly, tough soldiers, many were mostly homesick kids. Local families, ours included, would spend time with them. Luckily, the soldiers had petrol coupons and local families had cars; a good match-up. Our family took them touring around to see the local sites. We showed them Wannon Falls and travelled into the Grampian Mountains. Wannon Falls are not quite like Niagara Falls, but as a child I thought they were huge. Around 1971, I took my first trip to Niagara Falls and in looking at that mass of water pouring over those majestic cliffs, I thought, *perhaps the Wannon Falls were not all that big after all.*

We had two extinct volcanoes in the area and sometimes we had a picnic and climbed to the top for a wonderful view of the surrounding landscape.

Sometimes we all piled into our Plymouth car, Mum and Dad in front, the boys in back with my sister and me on their laps. The car was old and had to be cranked to start it. My father showed the marines how to get her going and they would crank away till the motor turned and off we went.

I think they liked being part of a family for two weeks, and I imagine that my sister and I may have reminded them of their own kid sisters. They were always so nice to us and so polite. There was never a moment of trouble and those were delightful times in my memories. They were a bright spark in our war years. They lifted all of our spirits.

An Unexpected Guest

A little while after the battle of Guadalcanal, Italy, surrendered in North Africa. Thousands of captured Italian soldiers were shipped to Australia until the end of the war. They were housed in prisoner of war camps, but Australia wasn't set up to house so many of them. The Government decided they should work on the farms instead of the overcrowded camps. They were especially needed to fill the void left by our own Australian sons who had joined the military. We were a large country in area but with a small population; only about 14 million people. My father was asked to house and feed one of the Italian POWs in exchange for his help with work on the farm.

"Girls, we are going to have a visitor, one that will be staying with us for a while."

"Who is it? Who's coming Father?" I asked.

"An Italian boy, a soldier. His unit surrendered to us in Africa and we have been asked to teach him to farm and house him till the war is over."

"A prisoner?" my sister replied with both fear and excitement in her voice.

"Yes, but an Italian one. I'm sure he will be quite nice." said Mother, always optimistic. Luckily, she was right.

In 1943, Umberto Revera – Berto for short--arrived. He wore a burgundy red uniform and spoke not one word of English. It also turned out that he knew nothing about farming. He was a city boy, but he was willing to learn and had a pleasant way about him.

He had been told that there were two young girls in the house and, like a good Italian, he brought gifts for each of us. Jewelry! He made us trinkets out of coins. My gift was a little ring he had fashioned out of a silver sixpence. I was allowed to wear it to church on Sundays and it was my most prized possession. I kept it in a special little box and I have kept it all these years, all of my life.

Berto was an unexpected visitor but as it would turn out later, a much needed one.

Chapter 3

The Worst Day of Our Lives

Berto and the Family

Berto settled in with us quickly. He was happy to have a warm bed to sleep in and good food to eat and we treated him like another member of the family. Though he knew nothing about farming or tending sheep, being a city boy from Florence, he was attentive to my father and did what he was told without question. I think he admired my Dad and wanted to please him.

Berto slept in the workman's room my father had built for the seasonal workers who came to help with the sheep. It was near our garden and offered a comfortable bed and place for Berto, much better accommodations than he had at the camps. He slept out there, but he ate his meals with us. He enjoyed the wonderful lamb we cooked which was something new to him and all the fresh vegetables from our garden and never complained about the lack of pasta. After he got to know us well, he actually made a few pasta dishes for us and we found them most enjoyable. They were quite different, just as he was with his dark hair and eyes and olive complexion. He was a nice boy and we were all quite fond of him.

Little by little, we taught him English and he taught us a bit of Italian. The authorities would come around every couple of weeks to check on him, but there was never a problem or complaint. He was a friend, not a prisoner in our eyes.

The summer after Berto arrived was the driest summer ever recorded in Australian history. There was a severe drought in Victoria and because of these facts, the bush fires began to happen.

Bush Fire - 14th January 1944: The Worst Day of our Lives

We heard word of the fires spreading. There were articles in our local paper and reports that came over the radio at night. We didn't feel a need to be too concerned just yet. Seasons in Australia are at opposite times to those in the northern hemisphere. December to February is our summer, our hottest months.

Our family's calm and peaceful life came to a sudden stop on 14th January 1944. I was just nine years old and, yet, all these many years later, I still think of that day and relive every moment of it.

It was what Mum called "a bad fire day." A hot north wind was blowing and it was mid-summer so the grass was high and dry. Mid-morning, a phone call came from the post mistress and confirmed our fears.

"There's a bad fire the other side of Hamilton", she said.

Mum hung up the phone and ran to get Dad who was working in the barn.

"There's a fire just the other side of town. We need to be prepared," she told him.

He nodded his head and set to work trying to prepare for the worst.

The whole Western District of Victoria was very fire-conscious. It was prime pastoral land with lots of dry grass, eucalypts, and pines trees. There was no Country Fire Brigade-- only a poorly-organized, voluntary band of willing workers, mostly farmers. My father was one of these men. In fact, he was Treasurer from 1935-1942, Secretary from 1942-1955, and Captain of the brigade from 1955-1965.

When the big bell in the church tower was rung to summon fire-fighters to the church, Dad had to leave us as duty called. Though we lived two miles from the church, we could hear the bell ring. This was an eerie sound and meant, "be alert." On this particular day, we knew immediately that it was a bad situation. The hot north wind and dry conditions meant instant action needed to be taken. Soon men arrived ready to set off with equipment in cars and trucks.

Before he left to fight the fire with the other volunteers, Dad told Mum to listen to the radio.

"If things get worse, you must take the girls to the dam." he told her. Seeing the frightened look in all of our eyes he added, "Not to worry my loves, we'll get it under control."

With that, my Dad and Berto went with the others, climbing quickly into our old Plymouth, following the rest of the volunteers to the source of the fire.

My sister and I were quite scared and stuck to our mother like glue. We could not imagine what a bushfire coming near our home might be like, or what devastation it could bring.

"Alright girls, we're going to be prepared just in case. Let's pack some clothes in our suitcases in case the worst happens," she said.

"What would be the worst Mum?" my sister asked timidly, afraid to hear the answer.

"Well, it is possible the house could burn down and we must be prepared for that."

Seeing our upset faces she added, "But, we hope for the best and pray to God to protect us. We'll be alright, but hurry."

We set about to pack our things. I sneaked a small doll into my case when Mum wasn't looking, one of my favorites and not without a little guilt of having chosen that one, leaving the others to fend for themselves. Once the cases were packed, Mum told us to take them to the edge of the dam and we watched as she turned the hose sprinklers on the huge flower garden and lawns. As it turned out, that very smart action would be the thing that saved the house from burning down.

When we got near the dam, Mum told us to switch the windmill off as it was spinning so fast it could break down. It was high up on the mound at the edge of the dam and spinning faster than I had ever seen it go. We set our cases down on the edge of the dam, switched off the windmill, and then headed back to the house to wait.

Father and Berto Return

It seems that the fire was started by a coal train on its way to Portland. Hamilton was just seven miles from our farm. Sparks had ignited the dry grass on the side of the tracks and it was soon out of control, burning on the outskirts of Hamilton. The fire fighters began losing ground when the strong wind changed to a westerly direction which meant our house wound up right in the path of the fire.

Dad and Berto had to leave their efforts at the fire. Dad told us the story later. They jumped in the car and drove as fast as the car would go for home and though he drove faster than he ever had, he had a hard time staying ahead of the fire. Black smoke was everywhere and they could barely see the road; the heat of the fire raging at their backs.

My mother soon realized this was becoming very serious. She had us pray for our father and Berto and waited anxiously pacing in front of the farmhouse, eyes peeled on the road, watching for our car. When it finally pulled into the yard, Dad screamed to Mum to take Eleanor & me to the dam as the fire was right behind him. He sent Berto with us to help protect us, but Dad stayed back to put the sprinkler on top of the car to try and save it.

The black smoke was almost suffocating as we jumped into the dam. We could see the flames coming straight for us and screamed for Dad, but there was no sign of him. Berto paced at the edge of the dam looking as though he wanted to run back for father. We were all in the water, screaming and crying for Dad. What if he didn't come?

Please God, save father, was all I could manage to think and I repeated it over and over in my head.

At long last, we saw him coming, bursting through the pine trees, running at full tilt, just as the burning embers were starting to land in the water of the dam. The fast-moving fire was fueled by the tall dry grass and the hay stacks in the path to the house. Any of our exposed flesh not in the water was catching alight from the flying embers, burning our arms, heads, and hair. Dad and Mum kept pushing us under the water of the dam to stop us from burning. We were so frightened, certain that we wouldn't survive. Poor Berto was saying, "Momma Mia," and crossing himself as he was a devout Italian Catholic. The fire continued to rage and we were shivering, and shaking from the shock of what was happening to our beautiful farm.

"Am I going to be burned to death by that ugly Australian bush fire, or am I going to drown in the dirty dam water where the sheep drank and pooped?"

The neighbors, a mile away on a hill, saw the flames through the smoke and later told us that they were sure we would all be dead. The fire hadn't reached them yet as there were several tongues of fire going at different speeds and running parallel to each other.

The double row of pine trees between the dam and the house ignited as if kerosene was thrown on them. Finally, after 2 1/2 hours, the longest hours of any of our lives, the fire had done its worst. My father announced that he was going to leave the dam to check on the house and sheds. He instructed us to stay in the dam and we obeyed. Berto stayed with us, continuing to douse us with the water when stray embers flew our way.

When father got to the house, he found it burning in several places. He told us that he had to pull out window frames with his bare hands, and throw burning mats off the verandah, throwing buckets of water wherever he could to save the house.

He saw that the grain shed was already burnt to the ground as were the machinery sheds, the stable full of chaff, with our six Draft horses inside.

Next, my father went to check on the shearing shed. As far as he could tell it was still standing, so he went up the stairs, opened the door and was greeted with a wall of flame. He was thrown backwards, and with that the shed collapsed and fell in a heap of burning timber and iron. It had been burning from underneath where the sheep droppings had ignited. What a miracle that he didn't go earlier into the building.

The fire destroyed all the fences, sheds, machinery, sheep, horses, cows, chickens, and our pig. One of the large tank stands crashed to the ground.

We lost everything except the house.

When Dad finally came back to the dam to see if we were okay, he brought back some fresh water, so Mum knew in that moment that the house was still there. She promptly fainted, but recovered as Dad gently patted her cheeks and got her to drink some clean water.

When finally we were able to climb safely from the dam, we trudged slowly back to the house. It was a terrible sight to see; black ground everywhere as everything was still smoldering.

Chapter 4

We Rebuild

Amazingly, the sheep dogs found shelter somewhere and were alive. We didn't know where they were hiding as everything around us was burned, but we were happy to see them. The house yard was surrounded by pine, eucalyptus, and cypress trees which were all burned. The yard had been a wonderful shelter from the strong winds. When we got back to the house we sat in shocked silence on the front verandah. We couldn't go inside at first because the house was full of smoke and soot.

The police from Hamilton finally allowed the roads to open, though houses were still smoldering from the fires. Family members were eager to reach their relatives. Our uncle, my father's brother, had been shopping in Hamilton, and when he could finally get through the road blocks he came to the house but couldn't find us. He was calling out "Ben, Ben, where are you?" He was so relieved to find us alive on the front veranda. My grandparents were anxiously awaiting any news of us, praying we were still alive. As soon as they were able to navigate the roads, they, too, came out to the farm. They were shocked and overwhelmed with relief when they found us.

All of the phone lines were down. All the bridges in the surrounding areas were gone. The post office, grocery store, confectioner house, and many houses in the community surrounding the Tarrington area were gone.

Embers were still burning around our house and there was a danger of the wind blowing smoldering embers into the house and setting it alight. So, our grandparents insisted we go with them to Hamilton to spend the next few nights. Our car was flooded from the sprinkler so we had to leave it on the farm. My father was having trouble seeing because his eyes had suffered damage so my grandparents took him to the Hamilton Base Hospital to have them check him out. Later in life, his eyesight deteriorated so much that he was declared legally blind in his mid- 80s, which we believe was caused by the fire. Also, as a result of the fire, Eleanor and I had to have our tonsils removed. The smoke had affected our throats so badly and the doctors thought it best to remove our tonsils to avoid future troubles. Eleanor and I had terrible nightmares for weeks after the fire and used to scream out loudly and wake our parents. It took a long time to get over the horrible ordeal we had experienced at such a young age. To this day, more than 70 years later, I can still see the flames as if the whole ordeal had happened yesterday.

As we drove through Tarrington, we were shocked to see so many houses burned to the ground. We knew everyone who lived there, so it was very sad to see such destruction.

The aftermath was another, yet different kind of experience. The village of Tarrington had been almost wiped out. The grocery store owner's mother who was living with his family, died when the house collapsed. We heard she went back into the house to collect some things while the rest of the family had all escaped to the church for shelter, as did many other people.

About forty homes were lost in the Tarrington district and another seventy elsewhere.

There were burned, dead, and straying sheep and cattle all over the countryside. People were in a state of shock and consternation. The fire finally burned itself out miles away in the stones that came out of the crater from the eruption of a local mountain. Later, the Governor of Victoria came to visit the area. Our first wooden church building survived the fire, but the newer bluestone church was destroyed. The parsonage and the big church built in 1928, where many people sheltered, were still standing. Even the old Historic Hotel built in the 1800's was saved, but eventually torn down in the 1950's when it was too dilapidated to refurbish. The loss to the community was incredible. Not one family was totally spared.

Everyone lost something.

Despite everything, all the destruction and loss, many prayers of thanksgiving to be alive were said in church on the Sunday following the fire.

Back to the Farm

We stayed in Hamilton with our grandparents for several days until things calmed down at the farm. Our grandparents were very kind to us and took good care of us knowing that we'd all been through quite an ordeal. We were all still in shock and no one spoke much. We slept and ate and took walks. Mother and father eventually said it was time to go back home and we climbed into my grandparents' car, a solemn group ready to face what lay ahead.

Going back to the farm was very sad as we had lost so much, but were very thankful that we still had our house. At the time, we kids weren't really aware of how bad things were. Somehow, our parents remained positive and that carried over to us. I remember my mother shedding a few tears from time to time but she never broke down or quit and my father simply set his sights on the work ahead. I never saw him complain or weaken. He just went full-tilt toward rebuilding the farm and our lives.

The loss of the animals in such a brutal way was a bitter pill to swallow. It was difficult to think of them suffering such a terrible end, but we had so much to do that those thoughts had no time to fester. We had each other and our home and we all pitched in to make things right as soon as possible.

A peat swamp two miles away caught fire and blew soot and black dust into our house almost every day. It carried that strong and awful peat smell which made matters worse. Because it was still war time, Dad had to sign papers in triplicate to buy even a hammer. All his tools were gone.

How do you get started?

Many farmers were able to purchase a lend-lease truck from America (the only ones available). Whether he wanted to or not, Dad had to start modernizing the farm as his old methods of farming were gone. He purchased a tractor, but because of the war, no rubber was available for wheels. So, steel ones were used instead, which made deep ruts everywhere he drove the tractor across the farm. We replaced the wooden fence posts with cement ones. After school, we would all help string wire through the post holes and secure them to the posts; a long and tedious job, but it had to be done. All the dead trees had to be removed before we could plant new ones. Berto learned to use an axe to cut them up. He thought this was a fun task until one day he almost cut off his leg.

The cow shed was the first to be erected, followed by buying a cow. Sheds had to be rebuilt for the new machinery. For the shearing shed we took the old corrugated iron and beat the dents out of the sheets to straighten them as much as possible, also straightening as many nails as we could find laying about. The wood for the shed had to be purchased as that had all burned to ashes in the fire. The Government gave us some Army issued khaki colored paint to cover the black iron that went on the walls and roof. It is still like that to this day. Berto was a big help to Dad with all that had to be done. We were so grateful to have him and he, like Dad, never complained or let us down.

It was several years before we could have sheep again. First, the grass had to grow back. Dad purchased a few sheep at a time as the paddocks were fenced to keep them on our farm. It took my father many years to get back on his feet again. There was so much to be done, and even so, it was never the same.

Berto Leaves and the Work Continues

About a year after the war was over, Berto and all the Italian prisoners were sent back to Italy. He expressed mixed feelings about returning not knowing what he and his friends would find at home. We gave Berto a big sendoff. Mother made him a special dinner and we promised we would try to come see him in Italy someday. We waved goodbye wildly, running after the car, as he drove away. It was sad to see him go and I knew my father would miss him and all the help he gave us.

My father taught me to drive the big truck even though I was not old enough to have a driver's license. I only drove around the farm, not on the roads. The truck had a stick shift and I felt very powerful sitting on a cushion trying to see out of that big thing. My feet barely touched the pedals but I got the hang of it and loved driving back and forth across our property. I was proud to be able to help him and he would send me off in the truck to fetch things he needed while he continued to work.

The Government asked the farmers to grow flax as it was a crop that hadn't been planted in our area before the fire. Ironically, later, after the war it was exported to Japan, our attacker years before. Since we couldn't do much else with the land, father complied and we worked some of our land for a crop of flax.

Before the fire we had all the food we needed. Meat, eggs, milk, vegetables, fruit, etc. were all available without leaving the farm. We were self-sufficient and had been my whole life. I guess I took it for granted that we always would have all we needed. It was quite a shock to have to go to the butcher shop to get our meat, to the green grocery to buy food with the limited amount of coupons we received. I must say, on the plus side, we enjoyed eating sausages and fish for a change instead of lamb.

All the farmers were struggling to make ends meet during these rebuilding years. I remember Dad making many trips to the bank for a loan to keep us going until the crops and sheep would start producing again. It must have been incredibly hard for my parents to start over.

Despite all of our efforts, after the fire the farm never was the same.

I must mention that, like most of the farmers then, we had no insurance for our farm.

So, we were BROKE!

Chapter 5

Continuing My Education

About four years after the fire, electricity came out into the country and that made life so much better for our family. The war was over and things were looking up. Mum and Dad built onto the small farm house adding a large kitchen, dining room, den, another bedroom and shower. They added lots of built-in cupboards and a new coke stove for the many meals my mother prepared. Coke is a derivative of coal and burns well and for a long time and is far less expensive than coal. Coke is still used as a fuel source in Australia today in some of the big factories. They also purchased a refrigerator and an electric radio, but the phone was still on a party line, operated by the post-mistress. Some things took longer than others to change.

Meanwhile, life had begun changing for Eleanor and me.

School Days

I attended the local Tarrington Church School from grade 1 through grade 8. With the war and then the difficulties of the fire, school was a great outlet and a happy place for my sister and me. It was a small school of about sixty students with only two teachers who between them taught all subjects in all eight grades. Each morning we gathered in front of the school, the flag was raised, and we sang "God save the King," and then recited the pledge of Allegiance to God, King, and Country. We loved our school and our teachers and our parents believed that girls should get a good education. We were very fortunate. We walked the two miles to school through my father's paddocks. On the way home Eleanor and I picked "buttercups" (wild yellow flowers) to take home to our mother. As we got older, we rode our bikes on the road to school.

Even during the war, we had a good deal of fun. One of my favorite events was the annual school picnic. We celebrated the picnic with races and games on my grandfather Noske's farm which was only a short distance from the school. The school children raised money for the picnic by riding our bikes to the neighboring farm houses and asking for donations. People were always willing to contribute. The school committee ladies bought the prizes for the races. I was quite a runner back then and won the 100-yard dash; the hop, skip, and jump race; and the three-legged race with my friend. My grandfather Noske made a see-saw which was constantly in use. He also made and erected a merry-go-round for the children to use the day of the picnic.

Music Education

Our parents wanted us to learn to play the piano. Lessons were given to us by Dorcas Noske in Hamilton who, despite the same last name, was no relation to us. They were friends of my family. The house, called *Myrniong*, was a very large, beautiful, two-story mansion with lots of rooms, a lawn tennis court, impressive gardens, and many fancy cars. They owned a great many acres and had a staff to service the property.

When I went for my lessons, I went to the heavy, carved, wooden doors at the entrance where a large St. Bernard dog would greet me. He always slobbered all over me and I hated it. Among the many rooms in the mansion were two beautifully decorated music rooms and in one stood a grand piano. I was not a musician. Dorcas tried very hard to teach me, but failed. Eleanor, on the other hand, was very accomplished and later played the piano and organ in several churches she attended. I managed to learn enough to be able to read music, which was very helpful when singing in choirs. I much preferred sports, however, and learned to play tennis on our church courts.

The Noskes travelled to Melbourne to engage many artists to visit our town to play and sing at the Hamilton Town Hall. After the recitals, the musicians treated us to more of their talents at *Myrniong*. The E.B. Noske family were very generous people and, when our large new brick church was dedicated in 1927, they donated the pipe organ.

Moving on to College:

After completing eighth grade, I attended Concordia College, a co-educational boarding school in Adelaide, South Australia. College in Australia is equivalent to high school in the United States. Only a small group of my classmates went away to college. Most went to the local high school in Hamilton. Buses picked up students in the surrounding area to transport them to the high school. Many of the girls did not go past the eighth grade, but simply went to work on their family farms until they met someone and got married, typically to farm boys from the area.

Eleanor went to Alexandra College in Hamilton. Our parents preferred that we attend religious schools over public high schools. They decided I would go to Concordia College which was a Lutheran co-education boarding school in Adelaide, South Australia. My mother's cousins had attended Concordia and found it to be a good school and a pleasant experience, so off I went.

I was very young, just twelve years old, and was quite homesick at first. We travelled by train 360 miles from home on the *Overland Express* which started in Brisbane, Queensland, to Sydney, New South Wales, Melbourne, Victoria, and finally Adelaide, South Australia.

There were about eight of us leaving Hamilton, arriving in Ararat where the train stopped to pick up passengers. It was early evening and it was quite cold in the winter time waiting for the train to arrive at 11 pm. The station staff had gone home to return later when the train was due to arrive. They left the waiting room open for us. It had a fire place, so the boys went looking for fire wood to keep us warm until the train pulled in to the platform We travelled all night, stopping at a few stations on the way, arriving in Adelaide early the next morning. We sat in "dog boxes," the name given to the small compartments with a passageway on one side of the train. There were foot warmers on the floor as it got quite cold at night. We did this trip three times a year, in May, September, and then for the longer Christmas holidays. Boarders came from as far away as Queensland, 2,000 miles from Adelaide. The students who would become church ministers attended Concordia Seminary on the same grounds as the College.

Concordia College

The girls wore uniforms and hats. We lived in a hostel about two miles away from the college, but the boys had their dormitories right on the campus. Our dormitory was an old, two-story, house, which was converted into a hostel but it was not very convenient. The girls had to take the two-mile hike to and from classes every school day. We walked two by two in a procession the boys like to call "the crocodile line." We walked all the way back to the hostel for lunch and then back to the college for afternoon classes. Meals were meager and not very good. I missed my mother's wonderful cooking. We got very tired of porridge or wheat bix cereal every morning for breakfast. We had our daily devotions at night, and then singing a favorite hymn picked by one of the girls. After supper (dinner), we took it in turns to wash and dry the dishes. On Sundays we walked to the Chapel at the college for church services. Instead of the mandatory tunic, blouse, tie, jacket and hat, we wore dresses with a hat.

We were locked in at night and slept in rooms with six or eight girls. We were not allowed to go out after hours, but some of the girls sneaked away to meet boys and were punished when caught. We had only two bathrooms for everyone. For the three years I was there, I slept in a sleep-out which is a veranda enclosed with louvers to make it a bedroom. The old house was always cold and drafty in the winter. It was not the most pleasant sleep experience, but it prepared me to rough it—a skill that would, oddly enough, come in handy later in life. College toughened us up quite a bit. We even experienced an earthquake in Adelaide. The old hostel shook and we were quite scared, but carried on afterwards as if nothing had happened.

Boarders like me, who didn't go home for the weekend, had to do their own laundry including sheets and towels. We got up very early to start the fire in the copper to heat the water. We were assigned certain times and days to attend to our own laundry. We hand-scrubbed the clothes, and then hung them wet on the clothesline. It was just too bad if it rained while we were in school. No matter what, we always had to be finished in time to get dressed and walk to the college for classes. We had a matron who was in charge of everything and kept us on task and on time.

On the weekends, when the weather was nice, the girls would spread blankets on the lawn of the hostel to sit or lie on and read, talk, or work on our studies. The boys would always manage to wander by to catch glimpses of us relaxing, but the matron would shoo them away as soon as she saw them. I don't know how they knew we were out there, or she sensed their arrival, but they all seemed to have it very well-timed.

Besides our regular studies, we were expected to learn to sew. The girls rode the tram into the city to attend sewing classes at the School of Arts. I was very good at sewing and made many outfits during my years at college and I later wore them to work.

Sports and Recreation

When the boys were not using it, we had gym class in the gymnasium once a week. The girls were not treated the same as the boys, but we did get to use that facility. The hostel had two tennis courts and four teams played on Saturdays against other schools. I tried out for basketball (net ball) and the coach wanted me to play on the "A" team. It was a big honor to play on the top team. We had four teams that played against other teams around Adelaide. We travelled by tram to go to the away games, which was a nice outing for us. For college games, boys and girls were divided into two houses, "Brown" and "Gold". The girls were placed on either team with no choice of their own. It was not exactly democratic.

On Friday nights we walked to the college for some relaxing times with the boys. One of our professors was a guest lecturer at Concordia Seminary in St. Louis, Missouri, USA. When he returned, he brought back records to teach us how to square dance (the craze at that time in America). They were fun times, and I took the craze to my home town when I left college. I taught the members at our Luther League Youth group to square dance, and they loved it. It was on one of these Friday nights that I met a young man named Hubert who was preparing to become a minister. He took a fancy to one of my girlfriends and he and I became friends, as well. He was a nice enough young man, but there was nothing more to it than that.

Even though the girls were not involved in track and field, we went along to the Intercollegiate Athletic Sports Day held on the Adelaide Oval (the main Aussie rules football playing field) to cheer them on. Our boys competed against other large boy's schools, but didn't perform very well. However they did perform very well in football, cricket, and tennis against larger schools.

Once a year we had a Brown and Gold Sports Day when the boys and girls competed against the other house. I was on the Brown House team. The girls had no training or practice time as the boys were always using the oval. My first year (1948) I won the Junior Cup which consisted of 75-yard dash, 75-yard skipping, standing broad jump, running broad jump, and netting the basketball. My picture was in the Brown and Gold magazine (year book) and I was so thrilled. In 1949, I won the Senior Cup, but in 1950 there was an epidemic of polio in Australia so there were no sports events that year.

I was chosen to type the articles for the Brown and Gold magazine which was published every year just before Christmas. I spent many hours and days typing after school. It was yet another honor for me as my picture was in the magazine again.

Our Family Grew

My sister Lynette was born in Oct.1946 while I was still in grade school. It was a big surprise, but we loved having a little baby join our family. I was the baby in the family for twelve years, but I didn't mind losing that position because I wasn't spoiled and I welcomed the new addition. We took Lynette for long walks in her pusher. She took the place of my favorite dolls. A real baby.

While I was in College my sister wrote to me and said a stork was going to visit our family again. That was a bigger surprise than the first announcement as I thought our family was complete. Nevertheless Elizabeth was born in Dec. 1949, arriving before I finished College. When I had time, I knitted both girls little cardigans and pullovers. When Mum went to town to shop, we usually pushed Elizabeth in her pusher and people thought the baby was Eleanor's because she was eighteen at the time. I don't think she was too thrilled. When Eleanor got married, my sisters and I were all in her wedding. We had beautiful dresses and everyone loved seeing the family of four girls in the wedding. But, my poor Father never had a son to carry on at the farm. As it turned out, none of us married farm boys or even would be farmers.

College Ends and Back Home I Go

When college days were over, I returned to my home in Tarrington where I was offered a job as a typist in a Chartered Accountants office in Hamilton. Only a handful of girls went on to University and those that did mostly prepared for nursing or teaching positions. There were not a lot of career choices for women in those days. I lived at the farm with my family and there was no other means of transportation to and from my job every day except to ride my bike (no speeds) the seven miles into town.

It was very hilly, and there was just a two-way road with only a gravel shoulder to move over to when cars came along. Heat, rain, and wind were the bane of my life. Depending on the elements, it took me about an hour to get to work. In winter, I started out in the dark and returned in the dark. So I had a small light on the front of my bike to show me the potholes and dips in the road. When the magpies were nesting, they would swoop down and try to peck at my head. I carried a stick to shoo them away. Not easy when you are peddling uphill against the wind.

After work I would stop at the local bakery to buy a fresh loaf of bread and pick up the mail at the post office. I had a small basket on the front of my bike in which to put these things. More reason to carry the stick to scare off hungry magpie thieves.

On one occasion when I was wearing my rain coat I had to lift off the seat to peddle harder to get up the hill. My coat tangled in the front wheel and I went flying over the handle-bars onto the bitumen road. I lay on the road for a time getting my coat out of the wheel. A car stopped to see if I was okay. He loaded my bike into the boot (trunk) and took me home all bruised and swollen.

I earned very little money, but managed to save half to deposit in the bank. I still had to do chores at the farm on the weekends. I didn't mind most of my chores except washing and polishing the linoleum kitchen floor, a task I truly disliked.

I worked in Hamilton for nearly five years. My sister, Eleanor, was married and living in Adelaide. She encouraged me to move to Adelaide and work there so I decided to take her advice. I lived in a flat with a friend and worked in a typist pool at the Army Southern Command Post. There were six of us and we just typed for the Generals and officers all day. It was a fun job. Later, I went to work for Ansett Airlines where my brother-in-law and his brother were working. There again I was a typist in the office.

College Reunion

One weekend, while still working in Adelaide, I attended a College Reunion. The reunion girls stayed in the old hostel where I spent my early years, and I reconnected with many old friends. On Friday night we attended the Adelaide Show and bumped into many college boys we knew who were going to the Seminary to become ministers. There I saw Hubert again and we had a nice long chat. He was continuing his studies in ministry and we talked about his plans and my work.

Back at the hostel to continue the reunion, I was approached by another young man I remembered from college days and we sat together chatting and catching up. He was very pleasant. We hit it off quite well. I guess I didn't see Hubert watching us like a hawk from across the room, but apparently he was quite miffed watching me with this other handsome young fellow.

I stepped outside with the young man and while we were talking, he leaned in to give me a kiss. Seemingly out of nowhere, came Hubert.

"Excuse me," Hubert said stiffly. "But I'd like you to step away from that young lady, she's my girl."

He was so serious and I stifled a giggle. The other young man surprisingly did not put up the least bit of a fight and, with a knowing nod to Hubert, he walked away.

I guess when things are meant to be, they're meant to be.

Chapter 6

Dating, Marriage and Life Begins

Neither one of us had a car, so we used public trains and trams so see each other. One of Hubert's friends started dating my roommate, so the boys bought a used motorcycle to get from the college to our flat to visit us.

Hubert would meet me in town after work and we went to the inexpensive "Shoppers Session" to see a movie. There were many beautiful movie theaters in Adelaide, some with organs that came out of the floor to play music before the show started. We often bought a sandwich or fish and chips and take our food into the theater.

Sometimes we sat on the banks of the River Torrens and watched the boats go up and down. Going to the beach was also a thing we loved. It didn't matter much where we were so long as we could spend time together.

After a year of dating in Adelaide and long-distance travel to visit my family at home, we decided that we would get engaged and married before he left for his first "call" assignment after graduation.

The boys at the Seminary were not allowed to be engaged or married until they graduated. It was one of the rules, but the professors expected them to go to their new parishes with a wife! That was a tall task.

How did the Head Master expect the boys to graduate, find a girl, get married and travel the next week to their new parish on short notice? IMPOSSIBLE.

Being a minister's son. Hubert had no money (they were poorly paid in those days). Fortunately, I had been a saver, and as he wanted me to have an engagement ring, we stopped at the bank on the way to the jewelers and I drew out some money to pay for it. He asked me if he could carry the money before we got to the shop to choose a ring. We still laugh about that today. I chose a small Australian sapphire with tiny diamonds on the side. At the same time we purchased a wedding ring and an "eternity" ring with tiny diamonds. It was a custom for the groom to present this ring to his wife on their wedding day.

Most of the boys graduating in early December had girlfriends and were also secretly engaged. Graduation day was held on the 4th of December 1955 in the Flinders Street Lutheran Church in Adelaide, South Australia. The church was built from bluestone from Grandfather Temme's quarry. As those were the days when girls and women wore hats and gloves to church, we all hid our engagement rings under our gloves, and when the service was over we took off our gloves and proudly showed off our rings to our family and friends.

Hubert's parents and brothers drove down from Queensland to Adelaide for his graduation from the Seminary and our wedding, a distance of 2,000 miles, camping in tents along the way. That was the first time I met them. His father and family stayed with his oldest brother in Adelaide. There were sixteen people in the family and Hubert's dad was number thirteen, so he had many relatives.

The Wedding

Prior to our wedding, I celebrated my 21st birthday with a party in the church hall with many relatives and friends in attendance. I received many beautiful birthday gifts and my wedding shower followed with even more lovely gifts.

I made my own wedding dress on my mother's Singer treadle sewing machine. It was a huge undertaking, but I managed to finish it in record time.

After Hubert's graduation from the Seminary, I returned home to make the final arrangements for our wedding. We planned our wedding while his parents were still in the South. Invitations were mailed for the wedding to take place on the 30th December 1955, which was to be held in the Tarrington Lutheran Church. We were happy Hubert's father could participate in the ceremony. He used the same bible verse that I chose for my Confirmation as the theme for his wedding sermon. In addition to Hubert's parents and brothers, a sister and brother-in-law, aunt and uncle, and several cousins came from Queensland for the wedding.

My mother was very good at arranging flowers and with the help of her cousin she decorated the church. The flowers came from our garden at the farm. I chose red and white for our color scheme as we had just celebrated Christmas and the girls carried red posies.

My friend Edna from grade school was my bridesmaid, while my youngest sister Elizabeth, then five years old, was my flower girl. Hubert's brother, Roland, was his best man, and my cousin John performed the duties of a page boy carrying the wedding rings on a satin pillow.

The wedding party arrived in two black cars with white ribbons adorning the hood. We pulled up to the church and the bells were pealing as we stepped out of our cars. My father accompanied me down the aisle as the organ played. Hubert waited at the altar, handsome in his dress suit, his brother at his side. We were both very nervous but we got through the ceremony and before we knew it, we had said our vows and were married.

Professional photos were taken at the home, church, and the photographer's studio. We had a lovely reception for 80 people at a restaurant in Hamilton.

My mother made a three-tier fruit cake (traditional in British countries) several months prior to the wedding. It was beautifully decorated by one of our cousins. I still have the top center piece which I used on cakes copied from the original for our 25th, 50, and 60th wedding anniversaries. Lots of beautiful crystal bowls, glasses, silver ware, dinner sets, etc., were given to us for wedding gifts. It's amazing to think of all these years that have passed and still being able to remember that day with such clarity.

At my grandmother's house I changed into my going-away outfit and then returned to say goodbye to everyone. After the reception, Hubert's brother Roland drove us around the streets of Hamilton trying to lose Hubert's college friends. They were bent on finding our wedding vehicle and decorating it with tin cans and writing *Just Married* in shaving cream. We managed to lose them but they later caught us and tossed confetti at us as we drove away.

The Honeymoon

We left Tarrington to start our honeymoon arriving in Ararat to spend the first night in a hotel. Unbeknownst to us, Hubert's brother Roland put confetti into our suitcases. When we got ready for bed, it was all over the floor in the bedroom. We could not hide the fact we were newlyweds.

The next day we travelled to Melbourne and caught the train for Sydney where we spent a couple of days. We toured the Blue Mountains, Taronga Park Zoo, took a ferry ride on the famous Sydney harbor, a boat ride on the Hawkesbury River and visited Bondi Beach.

Then we left for Brisbane where Hubert's brother-in-law Colin took us to his home in Kumbia. They did not attend the wedding as Hubert's sister Lois was expecting her second child. We stayed a few days, visiting other relatives, and then they drove us to Toowoomba to visit his mother and father who had returned from the wedding by then.

Hubert's mother was kind enough to take us around to be introduced to the many relatives. It was fun but quite scary to be on show to meet all the extended family members. I enjoyed all the tropical fruit, pineapples, and bananas that were plentiful wherever we went.

Before we left Queensland, Hubert was Ordained and Commissioned as a missionary by his father on Sunday 22nd January 1956. We arrived back at my parents farm to start our new experiences as a married couple and

Hubert as a brand-new minister. We would only stay there a few days, before we were off to our assignment. My mother, thinking that I would be going to a nice parish, bought me some lovely dresses. They turned out to be a blessing because every Sunday, at our mission, I would dress up, take out my good china, silver cutlery, and crystal glasses, all wedding presents and make us a nice dinner. This was a great way to lift our spirits.

Our First Commission

It had been announced on graduation night that we were to go to an Aboriginal Mission in the desert of South Australia, 1,000 miles from my home. Quite a shock, to say the least.

As my parents now had electricity on the farm, we took their old kerosene lamps, pot irons, washing board, wringer, an old kitchen cabinet, and *His Master's Voice* wet battery radio. It had to be charged often, so we could only use it for the news in the evening. We took anything that would be useful for us at the mission, including some old recovered chairs, a primitive glass cabinet for the living room, and an old table that had been used to make sausages whenever Dad killed a pig. Later, we stained it and used it as an office desk in the parsonage.

We stopped in Adelaide on the way to the Outback and bought some furniture from a discount store to be shipped to our new home at Yalata. We purchased a bedroom set, chrome kitchen table and chairs, and two beds for the spare room.

I have to say, my savings came in quite handy again.

Part 2

Life in the Outback

Chapter 7

Yalata Lutheran Mission
January 1956 - 1959

It was a great honor and privilege for Hubert to be ordained by his own father. The ordaining and commissioning was held in Toowoomba, Queensland on Sunday 22nd January 1956.

We soon set off, knowing our life would be very different. We had little idea of what was in store for us; the conditions, the people, and the adventures we would experience.

The Aboriginal Mission board supplied us with a utility truck to travel to Yalata. Hubert was appointed by the Governor of South Australia to be the first Missionary and Government superintendent to 600 Aboriginal nomads. This Anangu tribe with a *Pitjinjara* dialect were not coastal natives but central Australian desert natives. Caucasian explorers died in the desert for lack of water, but the Aborigines knew how to find water out of the roots of certain trees. At that time, Aborigines in Australia numbered about 1% of the population. Now, they represent roughly 3.3% of the population according to the latest census. Their status could be compared with Native Americans.

These Aborigines were displaced from the Ooldea area in the north of South Australian to be placed in a new mission called Yalata near the Great Australian Bight. This was necessary because the British and French Governments were about to test atomic bombs at a place called Maralinga. The government did not want the Aborigines wandering into the path of destruction so they moved them for their safety. This was no easy task.

Hubert's installation was at the camp where the Aborigines were living in the desert. It was 110 degrees, and, not being used to the extreme heat, I fainted. The Aborigines gathered around to see what the new boss and his wife looked like.

Soon I found myself, a newlywed, living 1,000 miles from my parent's home, and 2,000 miles from Hubert's parents. We were quite isolated, twenty miles from Colona Station, and 250 miles from the Western Australian border. I felt like a pioneer woman, but it was not in 1800s, it was the 1950's.

The Mission was given the use of 1800 square miles of land for the tribe of Aborigines with whom we would be working. To give you an idea of the immensity of that property, 100 miles of the Eyre highway ran straight through the property. Sometimes the Aborigines wandered off and we had to go and find them. We took a native with us to track them as they have amazing tracking capabilities. Typically, they never went more than 40 or 50 miles away because they wanted their government rations which we handed out regularly.

The Trans Pacific Railway station was about 30 miles north of us. The rails went 300 miles without a single bend. If you took that ride, you would see nothing but flat land, no trees, no foliage, no scenery. It was one of the most unexciting train rides imaginable. The Aborigines would come to us by train from out west. Often, when some of them were en route, we would hear an Aborigine say, "My brother coming." They knew somehow that their relative was on that train and headed toward us and darned if they weren't right. They would know if someone was coming, even on foot. It was a mental telepathy that was inexplicable.

Colona Station

The Australian Government gave the mission a million and a half acres of land for the 20,000 sheep, and a large woolshed with a ten-shearing stand for shearing the sheep. A large old house was provided for the station manager and his wife. They, in turn, provided a room for the mailman who travelled from Ceduna which was 130 miles from Yalata. The mail and supplies came from Adelaide by plane or on semi-trailer trucks to Ceduna. The mail truck brought our mail and supplies to the Colona station twice a week. Larger items came by boat from Adelaide to Fowler's Bay. The mailman stayed overnight and returned to Ceduna via Fowler's Bay, taking our outgoing mail with him.

We stayed at Colona station with the manager and his wife for about four weeks before we moved into our home which was twenty miles from the station property.

It was rather lonely at first. Luckily, a short time later, my good friend, Val Semmler from Concordia College, arrived at the station. She had recently married Erwin Dutschke, an airplane pilot, who had been hired to be the new manager of Colona Station. It was a nice surprise, as we had shared many experiences together and now would have the opportunity to have new ones. They arrived in 1956 with Erwin's Alpine Cessna, a four-seat plane. The plane came in very handy to find the sheep on the large property. The stockmen could then ride to the area and bring them to the station for shearing. It was a great time-saver.

There was another Lutheran mission 100 miles from Yalata near Ceduna called Koonibba. Koonibba was well established with a church, a home for children, a school, and both the pastor and teachers houses. Koonibba was a success. The Government wanted the Lutheran Church to have charge of the new mission called Yalata Lutheran Mission.

Arriving at the Mission

Church volunteers had erected two large tin sheds that we used as storage for government rations and clothing for the natives which were donated by churches throughout Australia. The lay missionary and handyman Ron Footner, who was married to the nurse Ella, lived in one end of a shed that had been converted into living quarters.

The Parsonage

A small asbestos house with no insulation for the heat, including 3 bedrooms, a bathroom, living room, dining area, kitchen, and a laundry room with a copper and two washtubs was to be our home for the next four years. Hubert used one of the three bedrooms for his study. He chose that room because it had an outside door so the aborigines could knock directly on his door when they were on the compound.

Two large galvanized water tanks were attached to the house for household use. Because the annual rainfall was only about three inches, the tanks were filled from outlying catchment tanks.

The house was built on limestone covered with sand. The truck with our furniture was parked on solid ground so it would not get bogged in the soft sand. Boards were laid down from the truck to the house on moving day. Aborigines came and moved our belongings into the house for us. They didn't talk much, they just steadily moved our things till the truck was empty.

The house had no electricity and only a wood stove for cooking which made the house very hot. I learned to make cakes from scratch. There were no packet cake mixes back then. I would open the oven door to see if the temperature was right for baking. If it was too hot, I left the oven door open for a few minutes till it cooled a bit. If it was not hot enough, I put on another log and get it to the required temperature. Surprisingly, I never had a failure. We ate breakfast early in the morning and then let the fire go out until the evening when I started it again to cook our evening meal.

We had a kerosene refrigerator which, when turned up too high, sent black smoke into the room. I found that to be very frustrating. The refrigerator barely kept fruit and vegetables cool enough. We had no fresh milk, only powdered milk.

For reading and listening to the news on the old radio at night, we used the old kerosene lamps from Mum & Dad. In the middle of the day, when temperatures reached over 110 degrees, we lay on the floor of the passage in the dark with wet clothes on our heads.

On Sundays I usually cooked a nice supper and used my silver cutlery set, good dinnerware, and crystal glasses, which were our wedding presents. I wanted to use them even though the conditions were not fancy. It was a way to give our Sundays a cheery atmosphere.

On washdays, I got up about 5 a.m. to avoid the heat of the day. I'd light the fire under the copper, fill it with sheets, towels, and clothes, and poke them down with a wooden stick. I used the old-fashioned scrubbing board, put them through the wringer into the rinse water, and lastly into the "blue" rinse, which was something akin to bleach, for the whites. The hot sun did most of the bleaching anyway. Finally, the clothes were ready to be hung on the clothesline.

I made a wooden chair for the basket so the clothes wouldn't get dirty on the sandy ground. Sometimes, we would have a dust storm, sending the dirt and sand of the dry desert terrain whipping around the house and yard. You never knew when this might happen and if I had the misfortune of hanging out clothes out on such a day, I would have to do the entire washing process over, hang the clothes up again, and hope for better results.

Hubert took an old five-gallon kerosene tin, soldered a rose shower spray on the bottom, and rigged up a pulley in the bathroom for a primitive shower. We heated the copper in the laundry, filled the kerosene tin with hot water, and took it to the bathroom. We pulled it to the ceiling, opened the rose to let the water out and then had to hurry to bathe and wash our hair before the water was all gone. We used much less water that way than we would have in a bath. As water was very scarce, we had to save wherever we could. We always showered in the evening so we would be clean and refreshed when we got into a nice clean bed.

We used the waste water from the house and channeled it into a drain in the back yard, which we filled with sheep droppings from the woolshed, and planted vegetables. The water from the house was actually filtered by the manure, taking out the soap. Consequently, we had fairly clean water to work with. Hubert enjoyed the challenge of creating a garden in the middle of the desert conditions of the Outback. The sheep dung was like fertilizer, and with a bit of effort, we had carrots, cucumbers, and tomatoes in our garden. This, at least, gave us some fresh veggies at times. Otherwise, tinned goods were used on a regular basis. With the few fresh vegetables, and our strange diet, it's a wonder we didn't get sick; a little miracle. We were young and healthy and could fight off anything in those days, I suppose.

When we went to Adelaide, I bought material to make curtains. I used Mum's Singer treadle sewing machine to make them as well as the bedspreads for the spare room. We bought linoleum and Hubert laid that in the house. Slowly but surely, it was beginning to feel like home.

As the ground was hard limestone, the holes for the phone line from the highway to the house had to be dynamited. The natives helped with this job. It was a big help to finally have a phone in the house. We still had to go through the operator in Fowler's Bay, but it made communication much easier. The natives also helped with a brush fence around the house, dynamiting holes the same way. The shrubbery gave us more privacy and a little protection from the wind.

Lamb that was slaughtered at Colona Station was our staple meat. Rabbits were also caught on a regular basis. We enjoyed rabbit and onion casserole. We tried kangaroo meat but didn't like it. It was too tough and tasted wild and too gamey to us.

We had many sudden sand storms and I swept up more dustpans of sand than I want to remember. The miserable sand worked its way into every nook and cranny of the house.

Another fact is that Australia has the most deadly snakes in the world. One day, a native saw the tracks of a snake go under our house and come out the other side. It slithered into the bush. He said it was a death adder. I admit that was pretty scary.

My mother's brother-in-law, Uncle Max Bunge, donated a set of batteries and a generator so we could turn on a light or two at night. A shed was built, and a Dunlite was erected. *Dunlite* was an Australian brand of small wind turbines used in rural areas. In Australia, in the 1950's, the Dunlite Corporation built hundreds of small wind generators to provide power at isolated postal service stations and farms. The first set of batteries Uncle Max sent came from Adelaide to Fowler's Bay on a boat. Very rough weather was encountered and the batteries were washed overboard. We had to wait another six weeks before they finally arrived on 23rd June 1958. Once everything was in place, we loved having some real light at night instead of carrying lamps to every room.

Our Exciting News

In 1956 on a trip to Ceduna, 130 miles from Yalata, I visited Dr. Myrna Miller who was the Flying Doctor stationed in Ceduna. A pilot flew her to all the outlying station properties in the outback to tend to the sick. It was the only hospital for miles around. She told me the good news that I was expecting a baby. She was a Lutheran Minister's daughter and became our good friend. Her sister Ruth married John Mattiske, a fellow Concordian, who was also the minister in Ceduna. It was good to visit them when we made the long trip from Yalata. They had a baby boy two weeks before our baby was born and we shared time together whenever we could.

Immediately, I started sewing maternity clothes, knitting booties and baby clothes for the new arrival. We were so excited, but a little nervous about having a baby so far from a doctor. The Lord was with us, and apart from having morning sickness, which sometimes lasted all day, everything went along quite well. The only small change was that towards the due date, I didn't visit the camp as often.

Penong was a small town with a petrol station and grocery store and pub. I was scheduled to go to the Penong Bush Hospital eighty miles from Yalata for the delivery. It was a large old house converted into a hospital, and it was staffed by two double certificate sisters under the leadership of the Anglican Church. Early in the morning, I woke Hubert and told him I think we better leave for the hospital. It was a two-hour drive to the hospital on the Eyre Highway and I did not want to have our baby on the way. There was dense fog outside and Hubert had to hang his head out the window most of the way to make sure he was still on the road.

When we arrived, the labor pains had stopped, but the sisters insisted I stay. Hubert left me at the hospital and returned to the mission. The pains continued, but still no baby. There was another patient there with me, but when she left, I was the only patient in the hospital. The sisters attended to the sick, delivered babies, cared for the infants, cooked the meals, and cleaned the house. They did it all. As my delivery was becoming difficult, the sisters called for the doctor to fly in and attend to me. I was so glad to see her, and finally, Jill, just 6 lbs. arrived at 12:20 p.m. on 28th April 1957. Hubert returned to the hospital when he received the good news of the birth of our baby girl.

My mother surprised me and flew to Ceduna. My husband picked her up at the airport and brought her to see the baby and me. I was in the hospital for two weeks. I was expecting to go home, but I ran a temperature, so I stayed another day.

It was so good to have Mum stay with us for a few weeks to help me adjust to the isolation with a new baby. Fortunately, Jill was a good sleeper, and had no trouble settling into a routine. I was able to breast feed her so didn't have to rely on artificial milk.

She was tiny, but started crawling very early and walked at nine months. We didn't have all the fancy baby items mothers have at their disposal today, but we managed just fine. She loved it when I put her on a blanket with a playpen on the front veranda, and played for ages with her few toys.

The "Dog Fence"

On one occasion Hubert shot a camel that was breaking down the fences surrounding the property. In early days, the camels were used by the explorers to carry their heavy load in the desert. After the explorers died, or the camels were no longer needed, they just left them to roam in the outback. This brings me to tell you about the "Dog Fence".

The dog fence was also known as the dingo fence. These sandy-colored, wild dogs were native to the continent. The "dog fence" was a squiggly line which ran 3,500 miles across Australia. It was first built by settlers in the 19th century, and was almost twice the length of the United States-Mexico border. In the late 1800s, ranchers first patrolled the fence on camelback. Our portion of the fence was inspected by the boundary rider from Colona Station. He was a staff member who did this regularly, and was away for up to two weeks at a time, camping along the fence. Sometimes he used a motorbike, utility truck, or went on horseback. He camped along the fence as he went on his patrol. He needed to stop the dingoes from burrowing under the fence to kill the sheep. Often kangaroos jumped into the fence and broke holes in the wire. The poor man had an endless job making repairs to the fence.

Chapter 8

The Mission Staff

Members of our church came to volunteer at the mission. They made cement bricks to build a house for Ron and Ella who had been living in the shed. It was a nice change and very important for them as they now had a little boy.

A school and showers were built. The children from the camp were trucked to the mission in the morning, showered, and changed into clean clothes for school. After school they changed back into their camp clothes and were trucked back to their families. They were taught the basic subjects of English, arithmetic, reading, and writing together with bible stories.

As more staff arrived at the mission, more houses were built. It was nice to relax and have fellowship with other Christian people. We were beginning to build a real community and it quelled the feelings of isolation we had felt in our early months there.

Hubert conducted Sunday church services, usually at Colona, as that was when the mail truck brought our letters and supplies from Ceduna. After the chapel was built, services were held at the mission compound.

In the evening, we often played cards with the staff to relax after a busy day with the natives. The popular game in Australia was 500, which is similar to euchre in America.

Life Around the Camp

The natives lived in rough structures called wurlies. They built them from branches often covered with tree limbs with tarpaulins or bags draped over them for shelter from the weather.

They lit a small fire in the middle of their huts and cooked "damper" in the hot ashes of the fire. Damper is a kind of bread made from flour and water and it didn't rise very much. Kangaroos, wombats, and rabbits were quite plentiful for the aborigines to hunt when they were hungry. Their wurlies were often thirty or forty miles from the mission in areas hard to reach by vehicles. There were no real tracks and we had to dodge trees and stones in the way.

The Aborigines moved around frequently due to the cutting down of trees for fire wood. The animals being hunted for food by them also became scarce. The ladies walked for miles to the catchment tanks carrying 4-gallon buckets. On the way back, they put rags on their heads to cushion and protect them from the weight of the buckets balanced on their heads.

The Government provided rations of flour, sugar, tea in tea cartons from India, potatoes, and onions. We issued the rations to the head of the household once a week. I sorted the clothing that came from the churches, and distributed them to the natives.

On a regular basis, Hubert conducted devotions using filmstrips which were shown on a screen operated from the truck battery. It worked well and they loved seeing the Bible stories in pictures.

For baptisms, we turned a tea chest upside down, put a cloth over it, and filled a bowl with water from a water bag we carried on the front of the utility truck. On one occasion, while our backs were turned, the dogs drank all the water out of the bowl. When he performed ceremonies like this, to look more official, Hubert wore his black gown over his shorts.

Ella, the nurse, went to the camp with us to administer various medications or tend to any cuts and bruises and eyes that were red and swollen from the horrible flies that constantly swarmed around.

The young lads from the tribes would play marbles in the sand. It was a fun and relaxing activity for them.

There were water catchment tanks scattered throughout the property for the aborigines and the sheep. These catchment areas were large, above ground tanks with corrugated iron roofs to stop the water from evaporating too quickly. After we arrived, one of the tanks near the mission was named "Temme Tank."

The only way to communicate by phone with the outside world was a mile away on the Eyres Highway (a dirt road from Adelaide to Perth, in Western Australia roughly 2000 miles apart). We were given a portable phone in an old leather case. Hubert had to shinny up the pole, hook the wires to the lines and then talk to the operator fifty miles away.

It was quite an operation, but very necessary during the bomb testing to keep the aborigines out of the affected area.

The Aborigines allowed Hubert to attend a Corroboree (a ceremonial native dance). They decorated their hair with feathers from birds, put a bone through their noses, and painted their faces and bodies with white and red ochre. They danced in a circle, banging on sticks for rhythm. It was called a "Song and Dance to the Morning Star," a kangaroo dance. During the dance they played a didjeridu which is a hollow log usually 3 to 5 feet in length, and 1 and half inches at the top to 2 and half inches at the bottom. It is played in conjunction with clicking sticks together and the clacking of boomerangs for rhythm in corroborees. To explain it, it is blown into the opening to produce a sound, not melodious, but it works the Aborigines.

The older initiated men were called "Wati." They took Hubert into the bush where they had hidden the totem sticks (Law/Lore sticks) as women were not allowed to see them. They even allowed him to take photographs.

When an Aborigine died they buried their own and had a "wailing session" for hours, lying face down in the sand. Sometimes stripping off their clothes. We could hear them miles away.

Before they came to our mission the younger children attended school in Ooldea, a mission camp in contact with white people. Some of the younger men left the reservation and learned English from working on the cattle and sheep stations. They were often paid with cheap wine which they promptly drank until it was gone. This was not a good thing.

The aborigines taught us to sing "Jesus Loves Me" in their native tongue, "Jesus Mooka."

Jesus mooka nayalu

Nungata Bible watani

Tji jooka joola balumba

Djarna oorba ballaru nunga

Oorwa Jesus mooka

Oorwa Jesus mooka

Oorwa Jesus mooka

Nungata Bible watani

One man, "Sugar Billy," was using bad language, so Hubert told him that it was not appropriate to speak that way. His answer was, "When I bloody well get wild, I bloody well swear."

One day we found a dead baby at the back of the ration shed. It was left there on purpose so we would find it and take care of it. The Aborigine had respect for the Missionary and knew we would do the right thing for the dead child.

The Aborigines were excellent trackers. They could spot ant and beetle tracks that had crossed the bare footprints of a person and determine how long ago that person had walked through the area. When they went hunting, they could tell how far an animal was from them. Police used the Aboriginals to track criminals with great success.

The police officer from Fowler's Bay was a good friend, and at times he had to come to restore order in the camp. Occasionally he arrested someone, and put him or her in jail for a few days. It always seemed to be poor old Ida that was being arrested! She was a woman in her fifties, her skin tone was pitch black, and she was an alcoholic who often stole money. Sometimes we would pick her up off the road when we went to get the mail. Sadly, she would also be picked up by white men who took advantage of her. When the police called Hubert to say a woman had been picked up, he usually replied. "Is it Ida?"

And it always was.

Another interesting trait of the Aborigine is that they never point with their fingers. They use their lower lips, sticking their bottom lip out in the direction of the object or person in question.

If asked something like, "Where's Ida?" They would reply with lip pointing, "oba dere."

Once a young native man hit Hubert over the shoulder and back with a *waddy*, which is a short thick club made of wood usually used for hunting or fighting. He was tracked down and received three months in jail for this action. Sometimes their anger would simply well up. And they would take it out on Hubert perhaps because he was admonishing them in some of his teachings, but this was the only serious incident of actual violence we encountered.

Periodically, the Flying doctor from Ceduna flew to the mission to take very sick patients back to the hospital 130 miles away. She also attended to the staff if they were sick. The plane was flown directly to the patient and simply landed on the grass in front of the house of the person who was ill.

The Aborigines were gifted in making curios, weapons, and these tools for hunting. They made boomerangs, shields, and waddies, spears and woomeras, which were very clever spear throwers that acted as an extension of the human arm, enabling a spear to travel at a greater speed and force than it would if simply thrown. The people who visited the mission were eager to buy these hand-made items. The natives enjoyed spending their money in the store and were happy to sell what they made. The mission also arranged to sell the curios to the stores in Adelaide and they were very popular because they were a novelty and not something made in a factory. These things were made out of the wood of the local trees called Myall and Mulga.

Paperwork and Work Visits

Hubert and Erwin were asked to fill out many Government and Mission reports and forms on a monthly basis. They referred to them as "Swindle Sheets," as doing this was so time consuming and not very productive as far as they were concerned. But it had to be done.

They made many trips to Adelaide for Government and Aboriginal Mission Board meetings, conventions and conferences. They used Erwin's plane for the trips to Adelaide, crossing Spencer's Gulf. Erwin flew the plane at a safe altitude so if the engine failed they could coast to the other side of the gulf. It saved many hours that would have been spent driving the 600 miles.

They visited many other mission stations in Erwin's plane. It was a great way to cover large distances in the outback. A special trip was to Coober Pedy where the largest opal fields in the world are located. The residents there live underground to escape the heat of the desert.

Alice Springs and a mission called Ernabella were also on the list of places we visited. Ernabella was like our mission.

Alice Springs is a stepping stone to Ayers Rock (Ularu) where the monolith exists. It is 7-miles around the base and is now a sacred site for the local Aboriginal tribes. The unusual thing about the rock is that it looks as though it is tipped on it's side because the layers of rock are vertical rather than horizontal. It is possible to surmise that this happened due to the Flood.

In Alice Springs, there was a radio station that used pedal powered batteries. The Pedal Radio sound was transmitted by telephone wires. The man who invented the Pedal Radio taught lessons to children within hundreds of miles for the station owners and their children. It was called, "School of the Air." School occurred each day for a couple of hours. The station owner's wives would pedal while school was being broadcast from Alice Springs to their homes. The Pedal Radios came in handy during emergencies as well. If an emergency arose, the pedal radio was the best way to reach out for help.

Maralinga Means Thunder

The area for testing atomic bombs by the British and Australian governments was frequently visited by American scientists and Military Army personnel. In the 1950s and 1960s, 35,000 military personnel lived at Maralinga. There was a permanent airstrip, then the longest in the Southern Hemisphere, plus roads, a swimming pool, accommodations and railway access. Seven bombs were dropped there between 1956 and 1963. On 4th October 1956 a "nuclear land mine" was detonated at Maralinga, tearing a crater 140 feet wide and 70 feet deep into the earth. Yalata was only 100 miles from Maralinga. Sometimes we heard the loud noise of an explosion. Once, when a bomb exploded, we felt the rumble and it shook the house. The bombing was so close that it cracked the concrete tanks at the mission.

It was difficult for Maralinga to communicate with us when they were testing the bombs. Alpha was a go, and Omega was when finished. It was all very secretive. The fallout and radiation could have been very bad for the Aborigines if they had roamed into that area. It was not easy to keep these "walkabout" Aborigines from roaming into this dangerous area.

The Americans who visited Maralinga were fascinated with the Aborigines and flew down in their helicopters to see how they made their Aboriginal curios. They loved the boomerangs, spears, woomeras and law (lore) sticks. The Americans brought food for us to eat and we would picnic with them under the trees. They brought crayfish, caviar, turkey, cold meats, tomatoes, salads, fruit, strawberries and even ice cream. It was such a treat.

The Americans took us for a ride in their helicopters to see the Mission from the air. They watched the Aborigines throw their boomerangs and were fascinated when they would come right back to the thrower. They made many trips because there were always new American Army personnel and scientists coming to watch the experiments in Maralinga. They were all intrigued and excited to visit us and meet the natives.

After it was considered safe for women to go into this remote area, the officials invited Hubert and me and our daughter, Jill, as well as the station manager, Erwin, and his wife Val to visit this very secretive place. There were still some staff manning this remote outpost.

Since the station manager had a plane for four people, it was arranged that he would fly us to Maralinga for a visit. We were the first people to have this opportunity and the excitement of visiting the sight we had heard so much about. Jill was just 7-months old at the time.

When the small plane touched down on the huge, long runway, a jeep was waiting for us with a sign on the back that said "FOLLOW ME." We taxied to where two black limos were parked, and when we got out of the plane we received a royal welcome from the generals. Jill and I were asked to ride in the back seat with the general and Hubert in the front. Val & Erwin rode in the other limo. They drove us to the Officers Mess where they had arranged a delicious lunch. One of the soldiers took Jill and made a makeshift pen out of pillows to stop her from crawling all over the place. They gave her toys from the gift shop.

After lunch they took our men to see the large craters and equipment that were used for the experiments. Val, Jill, and I were taken to the officer's quarters and asked if we would like to relax and rest until the men came back from their tour. It was a wonderful experience, especially since we were the very first women to go into that area.

It was a visit I will never forget.

Chapter 9

Time Away from the Mission for Relaxation

The Mission Board provided us a small fishing boat with an outboard motor. We went fishing whenever we could at Fowler's Bay which was about fifty miles from our Mission. Fowlers's Bay was a small village with a couple of houses, a police station and post office. From the time Jill was six months to two years old, she would often sleep in the bottom of the boat while we fished. We caught snapper, whiting, rock cod, salmon and sharks. Sometimes we trolled for snook and managed a good haul. On one occasion we caught five dozen. We loved the fresh fish we caught and shared them amongst the staff.

One of the local residents caught many lobsters from his lobster pots under the pier. He invited us to join them on the beach for fresh lobster one afternoon. That was quite a treat. What a great way to spend a few hours relaxing after the hectic life working with the Aborigines.

Boats arrived in Fowler's Bay from Adelaide with supplies for the surrounding farmers and residents. Often the crossing was quite rough and they could not tie up to the pier to unload their goods because of the turbulent surf. It was, of course, out of our control, but quite annoying to have to wait for the next boat.

The mission at Koonibba also had a small boat, and the minister there loved to take us fishing and share the catch with us and his staff. We loved the fellowship we had with the teachers and other staff members on the compound; yet another great way to relax away from our mission.

The staff went spotlight shooting to catch kangaroos, wombats and rabbits to take back to the camp. I sometimes went with them as I was a good shot having learned to shoot back on the farm with the rifle my Dad had given me. Birds, mostly crows, would attack our fruit orchard and, to keep them away, I would shoot them down. I was happy that my father had taught me to be such a good shot as it came in quite handy in the Outback.

The meat from the animals we brought back to the camp wouldn't keep in the heat, so the natives would sometimes eat too much, which made them sick. So, the nurse had to treat them for a stomach aches.

Playing Sports with the Locals

Hubert and I played tennis in the extremely hot summers, and basketball and football in the winter with the local team. In the summer, the hottest it might reach was 118 degrees, and in the winter the temperature could drop into the 50s in the evenings.

Our home team games of football and basketball were played about fifty miles from the mission with away games as far as 110 miles from home. After the games, we changed our clothes and enjoyed a meal in their halls. We loved meeting the "locals" and spending time with them. Hubert was voted captain of the football team for two years. I played basketball in a tournament and won the trophy for the "best and fairest" out of six teams. It was a great honor. A few Aborigines played Aussie Rules football. This is played between two teams of eighteen players on an oval shaped field. You score points by kicking the ball and getting it between the goal posts, 6 points for each successful attempt. You aren't allowed to throw the ball, only kick it and you have to occasionally bounce it or touch it to the ground lest you are considered holding it. It really can't be compared to American football, soccer or rugby.

Visitors to the Mission

The Board of Aboriginal Mission members frequented the mission to see how things were going, and ascertain if they could help with improvements. They sometimes arrived un-announced which made it very awkward to plan meals on a moment's notice.

Many locals also wanted to see the new mission in their area and were very curious about the Aborigines that came close to their farms. We wanted to reassure them that we would keep them at the mission and that they would not be a bother to them.

Family Visits

In October 1957 my Aunty Alma (Dad's sister) from Horsham, Victoria arrived in her blue Morris Minnie Minor car. She had lots of advice for me regarding Jill as she was an Infant Welfare Sister and cared for infants all her life. Jill and I drove back with her to my sister's house in Adelaide. On her way back to Horsham, Victoria, Aunty Alma was killed in a car accident not far from her home. It was very sad as we had spent so many wonderful days together.

Hubert's parents flew from Toowoomba, Queensland for a visit for Christmas 1957. They were eager to see Jill and loved carrying her around the compound to visit other staff members. The natives gathered at the mission and Erwin flew Hubert's Dad, dressed in a Father Christmas costume, to land near our house. The Aboriginal children were so excited to see this unusual experience happening just for them. He had presents in his big red bag to give to the children. Hubert's parents thoroughly enjoyed their visit and told everyone back in Toowoomba about our life at Yalata.

My parents came with Lynette and Elizabeth in August 1958. We were thrilled to see them. We took them fishing, which my Dad loved. They enjoyed visiting the camp to see exactly what my life consisted of as they could only imagine it up to this time. We reassured them that we were handling this adventure the best we could and enjoying it. Life was very different, and difficult at times, but also very rewarding. Very few ministers ever experience the life we were living with the Aborigines.

Foreign Visitors

The most exciting visitor was Peter Townsend (Princess Margaret's former boyfriend) who was driving a jeep from Perth to Adelaide. Queen Elizabeth would not give her permission for Margaret to marry Peter Townsend who was the former Equerry to King George VI and

Queen Elizabeth from 1944 to 1953. He graciously gave me his autograph which is now a prized possession.

A German couple on a motorbike and sidecar loaded to the brim stopped as they were travelling around Australia. They were quite an unusual couple.

Another special visitor was Dr. Bengt Danielsson, a Swedish anthropologist. He was a crew member on the Kon-Tiki Expedition from South America to French Polynesia in 1947 led by Thor Heyerdahl. He came with his beautiful French wife, and they were very interested in our primitive Aborigines and asked us many questions.

Sharing Our Ministries with Congregations

The Board of Aboriginal Missions asked us to share our ministry with congregations in South Australia by showing our slides of our work at Yalata. We were well-received, and all were very interested in the work we were doing which encouraged us a lot.

Jill was just a baby when we returned to Tarrington, Victoria, for a visit. She was baptized on 16th June 1957 in the same church where her father and I were married in 1955. My sister, Eleanor, Lionel, and their son Peter came to visit for the occasion. We loved eating all the fresh fruit and vegetables from my father's garden during our stay.

Perth, Western Australia – October, 1958

For a change of scenery and a place we had never visited, we travelled to Perth, Western Australia. It was a distance of 1,000 miles from Yalata to Perth. We left on the journey in our utility truck, packed with a tent, stretchers, sleeping bags, kerosene camp stove, folding table, chairs, and tin goods. The road was an unsealed, graded dirt road called the Eyre Highway. Eucla, 250 miles to the border, had a small store, a petrol bowser, and a couple of houses. On the way, Hubert shot a wild turkey and traded it in for some steaks which were easier for us to cook. The store people loved it.

We travelled 650 miles to Norseman where we stayed the night. The next day we drove to Kalgoorlie which was a gold mining town. We toured the mine and camped outside of Perth. It was a nice campground and we had a lovely night. Jill was just 18-months-old and was very good. She slept in a small basket under the table between the two stretchers in the tent. For eating, we even took her small low chair with a tray table. We saw lots of movies at the drive-in which was such a treat for us.

We met the minister of the church in Perth and he asked us to eat with them that evening. The next day we attended his Lutheran church. We stayed the night in a nice campground near Freemantle which is the sea port for Perth. We took a ferryboat ride to Rottnest Island off the coast of Freemantle where we saw lots of wildlife, birds and seals. We continued south through the Kauri and Jarrah pine forests where there are some of the tallest trees in the world, and we went fishing in the Margaret River.

In Albany, we met up with two former classmates from Concordia College, Adelaide. It was great to be with them. They had a little girl Jill's age. We enjoyed a picnic on the beach and they took us to the cliffs where we stood and watched where the "Killer Tides" crashed on the rocks below. On occasions, a tidal wave swept people standing on the cliffs above, into the sea below. We travelled to Esperance where Art Linkletter had a sheep station. There were wild flowers everywhere including many not seen in any other areas of Australia. There were Kangaroo Paw, eleven different species in many colors and sizes; Waratah, the state flower of Western Australia, which is very beautiful; Sturt Desert Pea; Cowslip Orchid; Bottle Brush; Wattl, and Banksia.

Finally, we returned to the Mission much refreshed from our journey and filled with memories that would last a lifetime.

Saying Goodbye to Yalata

We left Yalata Lutheran Mission in July of 1959 for Elizabeth, where Hubert had accepted a call to a new town outside of Adelaide. In many ways it was quite sad as Yalata was our first call into the ministry.

We experienced so much during this time and had grown tremendously as a couple.

Chapter 10

Elizabeth, South Australia
July 1959 – January 1965

Hubert received a call to be the first pastor in a town called Elizabeth (named after Queen Elizabeth II) just 20 miles from Adelaide, South Australia. He was installed on Sunday 26th July, 1959 with five pastors assisting.

In December 1956, a building lot was purchased from the South Australian Housing Trust to build St. Peter's Lutheran Church on Main North Road, Elizabeth. It was a "venture of faith", as there were no members at this time. Elizabeth was built on wheat fields and the Elizabeth and Salisbury congregations became one parish. Salisbury was a well-established congregation just six miles from Elizabeth.

The nearby town of Smithfield was used to accommodate the English migrants who came to the area in the late 1950's. When they first arrived on ships from England, they were housed in tin sheds. As construction was completed, houses became available, not only to the migrants, but to anyone who wanted to live in this new community.

Slowly Elizabeth grew with a hospital, churches, schools, shops, government buildings, houses, recreation areas, and a train line into Adelaide. The church hall was used for worship services, meetings, youth groups, Sunday school and just about any public gathering.

Four times, the congregation moved us from one small house to another before they built a manse next to the church. They wanted to make sure the church was going to survive before they invested too much money in the mission. The manse was dedicated on 12th December 1960.

I have to tell you a story about the small washing machine we purchased. It just washed the clothes and that was all. It stopped working one day, and Hubert decided to take it apart to try to fix it. He is not a fixer-upper, but he tried as he thought it would save us some money. After putting it back together, he plugged it in and pushed the start button. All the power went out in the house. We went outside to see what was happening because the pole outside where the transformer for the street was located was sending out sparks. It put the whole street into a state of panic. He refused to admit it was his mistake. He had to call an electrician to repair the damage. Lesson learned!

The church started with very few members but it slowly grew as we went knocking on doors to see if anyone would be interested in attending our services. When we left after five years, there were 250 members. That was considered quite good for a mission congregation. Many young Lutheran couples were moving to Elizabeth as they could afford to purchase their first home and start their families.

A Ladies Guild was formed and I became their first President and later the Zone President for all of the Adelaide area.

When Val and Erwin Dutschke left Yalata they bought a house in Elizabeth. It was such a lovely surprise to have them close to us again.

Hubert went to the British migrant camp on a regular basis to teach Sunday school. The kids were quite a wild group and would go outside to throw stones on the iron roof and disrupt the classes. Later, a retired police officer, George Suffling, brought the boys from the camp to the church hall and played games with them to get them out of their parents' hair. He tried to teach them some discipline, though he was not too successful at first. On one occasion, the boys took the folding chairs from the hall onto the highway in front of the church and played "chicken" with the cars. George was tearing his hair out at some of the things they tried. He had so much patience and taught them a lot while under his care.

We were in Elizabeth only two weeks when Jill, just two years old, became sick with pneumonia. She was in the hospital for a week, and was disgusted when they put a nappy (diaper) on her as she was already potty- trained. When she came home, we played a game blowing a ping pong ball back and forth on the kitchen table to strengthen her breathing. She thought it was a fun game.

The Weapons Research Establishment operated by the South Australian Government was between Elizabeth and Salisbury and many of our members worked there.

They had a nine-hole golf course where we were allowed to play in the men's and ladies' golf leagues.

Hubert conducted regular church services at Woomera Village, three-hundred miles north west of Adelaide. This was another secret establishment in operation during the Cold War like Maralinga. It was named after the Aboriginal spear throwing implement, the woomera which extends the range a spear can be thrown. I was lucky enough to be invited to join him on one of his trips. The Woomera Rocket Range was a defense-controlled town with 100-200 people.

Elizabeth and Salisbury combined for tennis and basketball teams. I played in both, and Hubert played on the tennis team. We won many competitions. Jill was the mascot for our basketball team, and I made a little uniform for her in our colors. George was a very good coach for the basketball team, and we won several grand finals. We added golf to our sport and played on courses in Elizabeth and around Adelaide.

One member of the Salisbury congregation, Dale Krieg, was a swimmer and was chosen to join the team for the 1960 Summer Olympics in Rome. We were very proud of her and followed her achievements that year.

In Elizabeth, we purchased our first black and white TV as television had just started in Australia. Color came much later. There were test patterns on the TV until later in the afternoon when a children's program started. Programs finished at 11 pm when the three stations concluded with an epilogue by a minister from various churches. Hubert was chosen to be this speaker on a regular basis. It was taped prior to the airing, and he went to the station in Adelaide to record his message.

The members helped Hubert build a fowl shed so we were able to have fresh eggs. It was so good to have so much fresh food after living in Yalata.

As the congregation grew, so did the Sunday school in each location. New Sunday school rooms were built to accommodate the influx of children.

At 9:30 pm on 3rd June 1960, a baby boy, Michael, weighing 7 lbs., was added to our family. Again, not an easy pregnancy or delivery. A few months later, we drove to Queensland for a National Church Convention. We travelled with another family and camped in our tents on the way. It had been three years since we had seen Hubert's Mum and Dad in Yalata. They were pleased to see their new grandson. They were blessed with two other grandchildren born within 6 weeks of each other. Talk about babies everywhere.

Living in Elizabeth, we were able to go back to my family farm more often and enjoy Mum's great cooking again. Dad always provided us with lots of fruit and vegetables to take home with us.

We had lots of Queensland family and relatives visit us in Elizabeth. It was good to see them as the cousins started to get to know each other.

Lisa was born on 23rd March 1963 at 10 pm at the Lyall McEwin Hospital in Elizabeth. Again, I suffered with morning sickness throughout the pregnancy. I also became anemic and received iron shots daily from the doctor the last month before Lisa was born. This time I lost a lot of blood and needed a blood transfusion which kept me in the hospital longer than I expected.

I continued to knit all our cardigans and jumpers for the family and sewed clothes for the children and myself. Jill started kindergarten and loved going to school. It was a short distance from our house, so we walked together to and from school. When Michael started school they walked together with their friends as there were plenty of them in the neighborhood.

Dancing was in Jill's blood and she started dancing around the house at age three. When she was five years old, we enrolled her in ballet classes. She loved it and won the under-six competition dancing to recorded music and her own choreography. She had a natural talent which grew as she got older.

One of the members, Ern Lindner, helped us build a lovely rock wall in the front garden. We planted roses and flowers in the beds. It was our pride and joy and was much admired by everyone who walked by. We had a large vegetable garden in the back and grew tomatoes, lettuce, cucumbers, beetroots, melons, pumpkins, peas and potatoes. I preserved as much as I could as we entertained many members and visitors during this time.

Hubert was able to play cricket and football when the Old Scholars had their annual reunion. He loved getting together with his old classmates who lived in the Adelaide area. I enjoyed seeing my old friends as well. He was elected president of the Aboriginal Mission Board and made many trips back to Yalata with other board members. The roles were reversed as, this time, he had a different part to play. They drove the 600 miles which became a little tiring after a while on the same old dirt road. The Aborigines enjoyed seeing him again and flocked around him when he visited the camp.

We had several friendly stray cats hang around in our yard. Jill put doll clothes on them and took them for walks in her doll pram. The children loved to play on the lawn when the sprinklers were going and got very wet. This entertained them for a long time.

I became very involved in many speaking engagements and showing slides of Yalata. It was the first time many guilds learned about the place where they sent their used clothing.

I celebrated my 30th birthday at the Hotel Australia overlooking the "lovely city of churches" in Adelaide. My friend Val's father owned a winery in the Barossa Valley where Val grew up. It was about 15 miles from Elizabeth. Val and Erwin arranged to have a magnum bottle of champagne delivered and cooled at the hotel for my special dinner with Eleanor and Lionel, Val and Erwin, Pam and Keith. It was a very lovely evening and one I will always remember.

In February 1963 Queen Elizabeth and Prince Phillip came to Windsor Green in the city center of Elizabeth to dedicate this new city. We felt privileged to be invited and attend this historic occasion. We were seated on chairs in front of the dais. On Christmas Day in 1963, our church service at Elizabeth was broadcast over national and regional radio stations. An honor for our young congregation.

In 1964 we took the children into Adelaide for a special visit of the Beatles to see John Lennon, Paul McCartney, George Harrison, and Ringo Starr. They appeared on the balcony of the Adelaide Hotel opposite the train station. Everyone, especially the young girls, screamed and screamed. We had no idea they were going to be so popular. They hadn't even been to America.

The Barossa Valley, with 27 Lutheran Churches in a 9-mile radius, was famous for the many wineries owned by Lutherans in the early years. The immigrants from Germany and other parts of Europe brought their grape vines with them and found the perfect soil and conditions to continue the tradition of wine-making.

We said farewell and left this lovely city and our many friends in January, 1965, to start a new adventure in Glenelg, a popular beach resort of Adelaide.

Glenelg: March 1965 – April 1968

Glenelg is a beautiful beach resort city, a suburb of Adelaide, South Australia, on St. Vincent's Gulf. Adelaide now has a population of 1.5 million people and Glenelg 20,000. Glenelg is a *palindrome*, a word spelt the same forwards and backwards. Adelaide is nestled between the hills on one side and the gulf water on the other.

A wonderful wild life park, called Cleland National Park, Mt. Lofty, is the home to kangaroos which will come up to you when offering them food. There are also many koalas that can be held, emus, wombats, and other native animals peculiar to Australia. We really enjoyed this park watching these animals while having picnics with our family and friends. There are great views of the city from Windy Point especially at night when it looks like a fairyland.

The only tram existing in Adelaide today leaves Glenelg and ends in the city center of Adelaide. The children loved riding these trams whenever we went to town.

The Glenelg Lutheran Church was well established and together with the Warradale congregation formed one parish. Hubert's installation at Glenelg was attended by 550 people. It was a great day for everyone. We reconnected with many ex-Concordians who attended Glenelg and the Warradale churches.

The Glenelg congregation had large attendances for Sunday school, and over 100 attended Vacation Bible Study during the summer school break. The superintendent and teachers were very dedicated, and worked long hours to give the children a good Christian education.

The manse was just a few blocks from the church. When we arrived, the front garden was overrun with shrubs and bushes. There were fruit trees, a large fig tree, peach, apple, passion fruit vine and grapes in the back yard, which produced nice fruit for us to eat. We brought our fowls from Elizabeth as there was a fowl shed next to the vegetable garden.

We enjoyed seeing my sister, Eleanor, Lionel and their three boys more often as we lived much closer, now. Mum & Dad sold their farm to our neighbor's son Syd and retired in Adelaide with Lynette and Elizabeth who were still in school. Jill, Michael and Lisa loved seeing their grandparents on a regular basis.

As we were so close to the coast, net fishing at night was very rewarding with large catches of Australian King George Whiting, a very sweet fish. On one occasion. over 500 were netted and the "boys" brought them to our home. My husband woke me up about one-o'clock in the morning and asked me to cook fish for them while they scaled and filleted them in the kitchen. I finally went back to bed around 3:30 a.m. I'm not sure why it was always our house they ended up at the end of a night of fishing. Doesn't that just sound like men!

Jill continued to attend a ballet school, this time in North Adelaide. The teachers encouraged her as she was doing so well. She was very petite and had great arm and leg movements. She kept winning award after award.

The South Australian District of the church bought an old winery in McLaren Vale called Tatachilla. Many congregations used it for Sunday school camps, youth retreats, and family gatherings. Our congregations often made use of this unique facility.

Our parish had four tennis teams: two men and women, one boy, and one girl team. We played against other church teams in our area on our own courts on Saturday afternoons. We were often grand final winners with a celebration afterwards at our home. There was also a lawn tennis court next to the church for members to use.

Lisa started kindergarten and loved it. School uniforms in Australia were mandatory in public and private schools. So, off Jill and Michael went to their school a short distance away, looking very neat. The teachers walked their students to the beach for swimming lessons in the ocean. Jill and Michael learned to handle the surf well, even though the water was quite rough at times.

All the shops closed at noon on Saturdays and didn't open again until Monday morning. Aussie Rules Football took over sports on Saturday afternoons in the wintertime. There were ten games playing on ovals in the Adelaide area with 20,000 patrons in attendance at each one. It was huge. The Glenelg oval was just around the corner from our home. We watched their games quite often, but were big fans of the Sturt team, as many Seminarians from Concordia were selected to play with them. We attended a grand finale at the Adelaide Oval with 35,000 people where Sturt defeated Glenelg 24 goals to 4 goals. Aussie Rules football cannot be compared with American football, soccer or rugby. It is a very fast game and the players wear no protective gear.

Because some of the footballers were young Christian men, we invited the Sturt boys to speak at our church service, and they had lunch at our home afterwards. Michael loved it as he wanted to wear his long "double blue" socks all the time. They were the Sturt team colors. He was young and still wore short pants.

Our members owned two "Pop Eye" boats that took tourists for rides on the River Torrens. The river ran through the center of Adelaide with very picturesque scenery ending at the Zoo. We enjoyed many of these rides.

As Hubert was still chairman of the Aboriginal Mission Board, he had many visits back to Yalata. My Dad enjoyed going with him on one of his trips.

On 14th February 1966 Australia introduced decimal currency with notes and coins, marking the end of the British-style currency system based on pounds, shillings, and pence. It was all very confusing at first. There were many jokes going around suggesting that the government wait until all the old people die and then introduce it. Or, just let the city people deal with it and leave the country people out of it.

We loved going to the beach with the children and especially enjoyed Moana further down the coast. This beach had some great surf with big breakers where we could body surf. We could drive our car onto the wide beach without getting bogged in the lovely soft, white sand.

Hubert was invited to join the Army Chaplains Corp. to work with the high school and college cadets. We attended many parades and events..

He was elected to the Lutheran Hour Radio committee to arrange broadcasts for Sunday services in and around Adelaide. He arranged for Glenelg and Warradale to have them quite often. They were played directly on Sunday mornings, but we could tape them and listen to the services later at home.

In November 1966, Hubert spent two weeks near Sydney, New South Wales, at an Army Chaplains training camp. Military dinners were formal and "dress blues" were mandatory. A military band played during dinner while all formal procedures were taking place.

Jill entered a TV children's program contest called "Humphrey B. Bear." She won and was treated to a plane ride around Adelaide by Trans Australian Airlines. She had her picture taken with the person in a bear costume and it appeared in the Adelaide Advertiser daily paper the next day.

When the Royal family visited Australia we stood on the streets with hundreds of other people in Adelaide, watching as Queen Elizabeth, Prince Phillip, the Queen Mother, and Princess Margaret drove by. They were always very popular as she is still the head of the Commonwealth of Australia.

In 1967 Lois, Hubert's sister, Colin, and their three children visited us in Glenelg. The children enjoyed seeing their cousins, as they were older now and loved the time they had together.

A Call to America

Norman, a classmate of Hubert's and my cousin, was a Professor at the Seminary in St. Louis, Missouri, USA. He was invited to preach at churches in and around St. Louis as there was a great shortage of ministers in all denominations at this time. Centralia, Illinois, had a thousand members, and called many times but the congregation was still vacant. So, Norman and other professors took turns preaching there on Sundays. It was decided to call a minister from Australia and Norman suggested Hubert.

It happened in January 1968, while Hubert was attending an Army camp refresher course. A telegram arrived at the house to issue him the call to Centralia, Illinois, in America. I tried to reach the camp and asked if I could speak with my husband to tell him the unexpected news. When summoned to speak to his wife, he thought something bad had happened to me or to the children. When I told him why I was calling he was speechless.

The news was not met with a lot of enthusiasm from the church members. They loved his preaching, and how the congregations had prospered under his leadership.

At the same time Hubert was asked to go to Vietnam as an Army chaplain for the Australian forces. Before we left Australia, Hubert conducted the funeral service for the first Lutheran soldier killed in Vietnam.

However, rather than go to Vietnam, my husband accepted the challenge in America, as the experience could not be matched in Australia. We were expected to spend five to seven years in America, and then we could return to Australia.

Little did we realize we would again be saying goodbye so soon to our many friends we loved in this great city of Adelaide.

It doesn't ever get any easier!

Map of South Australia

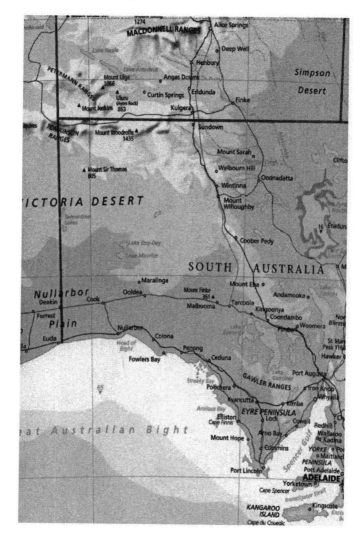

"Glenora" June's Farm Home

Tarrington Lutheran Church

Native "wurlie" (camp life)

Aboriginal secret totem poles

Carrying water to the camp

*Painted for Corroboree
Dance*

Kangaroo and Joey

June with Koala

June, Hubert, Jill, Lisa and Michael, 1968

Leaving Sydney, Australia, 1968

Lisa, Hubert, June Jill, Michael, 2015

Our 10 grandchildren

1955   2015

Above
60th Wedding Anniversary

Left
June and Berto (Italian
P.O.W) Italy 1983

Below
Ben and Vi Noske family
1991

Part 3

America

Chapter 11

Preparations for Leaving Australia

There were very exciting, but busy months ahead of us. We had to arrange for passports, injections, police clearances (to prove we were not in trouble with the law), x-rays, doctors health reports, etc. The congregation in Centralia, Illinois, and the Bishop of the church in America needed to supply letters to the Government that the church had called many times without success. They had to prove that this position could not be filled by an American pastor. To enter America legally, there were lots of hoops to go through before it was a "done deal."

I packed and stored my good china, silverware, crystal bowls and glasses in my parent's garage as we expected to return to Australia after a few years. We sold or gave away our meager furniture. Some of it went to my sister Lynette who was engaged and getting married in April 1968. Jill was a junior bridesmaid in her wedding and Hubert was performing the ceremony. We purchased some old "steamer trunks" and wooden crates for Hubert's library of books, clothing, and a few personal articles. The children were allowed to take a few toys, books, or dolls. Jill had eight or ten original Barbie dolls. She only took two with her, and she still treasures them to this day. Michael took his matchbox cars in a small case. Lisa took one of her dolls.

Family photos were taken at Mum and Dad's house with a professional photographer. Jill was eleven, Michael seven, and Lisa five when we left Australia.

Our farewell at Glenelg was the first television broadcast for a church service in Adelaide. After saying goodbye to the members, we left to have a family lunch with my parents and sisters. Many friends came to give us a fond farewell and wish us a safe trip to America. My parents gave the children lovely stuffed koalas to take with them on our journey to an unknown land.

We waved goodbye and set off in our car to drive to Queensland to see Hubert's family and relatives before leaving Australia. We did not know how many years we would be gone.

We sold our car in Toowoomba to a second-hand dealer. Hubert's parents were sad to see us go. His cousin John Kessler drove us to Brisbane, and then we flew to Sydney. It was the first time we had flown on a commercial airline.

Leaving Australia for America

It was decided by the Centralia congregation that it would be cheaper and better for the five of us to board a cruise ship rather than fly to America. The ship, "Iberia," was owned by the P & O Lines which was a British cruise company. We left Sydney on Sunday the 26th May 1968. Lynette and her new husband met us in Sydney and took us to stay the night at a minister's home. Robert Paech took us to the ship the next morning. We were in awe of the size of the ship, but it was very small by today's standards. It was just 30,000 tons with a first class and tourist class cabins. We felt we were in "steerage" as the cabin was small and on a lower deck with two double bunks and a cot for Lisa. It had a washbasin, but we had to go to the bathrooms down the hall to shower. The sign on the door said WC which stood for "water closet," or restrooms. The porthole was at sea level and when it got rough we were below the water line. It was still exciting to spend the next four weeks visiting countries we had never expected to see. Flowers and telegrams were waiting for us in our cabin.

It was the custom when a ship left the port for passengers on the decks to throw streamers supplied by the crew to the people down on the wharf as the ship pulled away from the pier. The streamers broke and dropped into the water. It reminded us of the old movies when passengers cruised around the world. When all the streamers were gone, we turned around and--no Lisa. We were frantic to lose our little girl before we even left Sydney. She was found shortly thereafter by the staff and was waiting for us at the dining room where we were to have lunch. Panic averted.

We stood on deck as we went under the Sydney Harbor Bridge and then out through the Sydney "heads" into the open sea. Sailing along the Great Barrier Reef, we passed New Guinea. We wrote cards and letters to our family and the pilot took them off the ship and posted them on Thursday Island. Apparently, a stowaway was found and he was escorted off the ship on the pilot boat.

On Sundays, the captain conducted church services in the ballroom. Apart from the current movies and dancing there was very little entertainment. We were expected to dress in semi-formal attire every evening for dinner. Fortunately, a model- friend of mine had given me some cocktail dresses when I left Glenelg. They came in very handy.

The weather was warm and sunny so we spent more time on deck during the day playing deck quoits and ping pong. Every day we took the children to the Arts and Crafts room where they were taught to make many lovely handcrafted items. They enjoyed the swimming classes when the weather cooperated. I was kept busy washing and ironing clothes. There was a laundry room on board with little washing machines.

For each meal on board ship, one parent had to accompany their children to the dining room as they ate separately from the adults. After the evening meal, I took them downstairs to bathe and prepare them for bed. We ate at the late service sitting with a young Jewish couple, Vera (a rabbi's daughter) and Dr. Mark Sperling. They had a little girl. They were going to America for two years to further his studies.

We were invited with a small group to the Captain's cocktail party in his cabin.

All the children on board took part in King Neptune's Court. The crew chased them around the deck near the swimming pool and, when caught, rubbed a smelly concoction into their hair and on their bodies. Lisa was scared. We watched as the parents laughed at the proceedings. It took ages to get them clean and for the smell to go away. Michael won the egg and spoon race and Jill managed to stay on the bar over the water and knock the other person off with a pillow.

On the day before we were to arrive in Manila, the crew decorated the children's dining room table with streamers and balloons. A cake beautifully decorated and a card and small pin from the captain were on the table when we walked into the room celebrating Michael's birthday while we were in Manila.

First Port of Call – Manilla in the Philippines.

We were greeted on the wharf with a band, and there were stalls with many beautiful handmade wooden articles and other souvenirs for the tourists.

After the Second World War, the Americans left their jeeps behind for the Philippinos to use. They were converted into taxis and called them "jeepnees". They were very bad drivers, but we hung on and survived. They took us to the Pananja Rapids out in the country where we boarded two long canoes with a man at each end. We got soaked in a downpour during a thunderstorm. They told us how some remaining Japanese had hid in the jungle for years, as they didn't know the war was over, and they refused to surrender. On the banks of the river we saw rice paddy fields, coconut palms, pineapples, mangoes, water buffalo, shanties, and women washing clothes in the muddy water.

In contrast, we saw many rich homes with guards at the front gate. It was strange for us to see police with revolvers on their belts. Our "taxi" had to stop to allow a funeral procession which was walking on the street. In the poorer areas we saw pigs tied up, children riding water buffalos, and people lining up to buy water. We stopped at an old church that had a bamboo organ. It was quite an experience for us to see a foreign country and how its people lived.

It was always fun to leave the ports as a band played, streamers thrown onto the pier, and people waving as we pulled away.

Arriving in Hong Kong

As we sailed into the harbor, people were begging for money from little boats beneath us. They had nets to catch the fruit the passengers threw, but the money went into the water and they quickly dived to catch the coins. They sang out, "Big one," meaning dollar bills.

Danny Yip, whose sister was a member of the church in Glenelg, met us and drove us to the Lutheran Roof Top Schools where we met Pastor George Winkler, the director. Danny then took us into the country to meet his mother and sister where we were offered a cup of hot water to drink. Our children gave us funny looks as much as to say, "Do we have to drink this?" We toured an open market where meat was hanging in the open with flies swarming around. Also, there were many duck farms, rice paddy fields and water buffalo tilling the land. It was interesting to see a very tall cement cross on a mountain in this Buddhist country. Hubert was measured for two suits that were made and delivered to the ship the next day. I purchased a knitted suit and some clothing for the children as everything was quite cheap.

The ocean terminal with lots of expensive shops was tempting for the tourists as they walked through on their way to the ship. We left Hong Kong with three bands playing on the dock.

The next day, a man had a heart attack in the shower and died. This was the second death at sea.

Japan – Kobe and Yokohama

When we arrived in Kobe, a number of Japanese students met us at the bottom of the gangway with their expensive cameras and asked if they could take pictures of our children. They took them aside and had them pose in different positions. Lisa, with her blond hair, was mobbed as they kept snapping pictures of her. She was such a contrast to the Japanese with their black hair. We took pictures of the students as it was quite a sight to see our children in such demand.

Public toilets were a challenge as they were just a hole in the ground and you had to squat over the hole. Occasionally we found a WC that had a door and said "Westerners." Always a welcome site as we knew this was for us.

When we arrived in Kobe, we were struggling with the language and a kind Japanese man who spoke perfect English offered to take us to the station where we caught the train to Osaka then Nara. We walked through a deer park to feed the animals and saw the largest wooden temple in the world with a huge bronze Buddha perched in the middle.

The next day we arrived in Yokohama. We were welcomed to the Japanese Lutheran Theological

Seminary in Tokyo by Dr. Kishi who showed us around. We had sandwiches and coffee with the faculty. He took us on a tour in an air-conditioned American Pontiac car. It was a nice change. There are 500,000 Christians in Japan. There was a "New Temple" built there for this new religion – an offshoot of Buddhism.

The following day we walked to the Yokohama Tower for a great view of the city and visited a Marine Museum and a US Naval Chapel. The chef on the ship had given us a chicken to take with us for lunch in the park. We saw large Koi and gold fish swimming in the lake. Japanese grade-school students were on a field trip and wanted to practice their English with us. They were not shy and kept talking to us while we were walking. One mother asked if she could take a picture of her daughter with Lisa.

Again, large crowds gathered on the dock to say goodbye to Japan. Bands were playing, and streamers blowing in the breeze. Five or six people missed the ship and were brought out of the harbor by the pilot boat. They were hoisted up the side by a bosons harness with everyone hanging over the side watching the embarrassed look on their faces.

That night we had an Oriental dinner and ball.

Next day, we toured the bridge. The sea was rough and Jill felt sick. The fog rolled in. The captain made an announcement over the loud speakers to say we needed to go to a place where we could stay for a few hours. The crew closed all the water tight doors, and put the heavy metal cover over our port hole which was mostly under the water line by now. We were lucky because we could go upstairs onto the deck through the galley. The foghorn blew every few minutes. It was quite eerie and reminded me again of the old cruise ship movies, but this time is was for real. We couldn't see anything beyond the railing of the ship. This lasted quite a long time.

Another death. During a movie we felt the motors of the ship stop and everything became very quiet. The next morning we read in the daily news that there was a burial at sea.

The water in the Pacific was a beautiful dark blue. Now we know why they call it the "Blue Pacific." We were crossing the International Date Line so we had two Mondays. It took six days at sea to arrive in Honolulu.

Honolulu, Hawaii

We stayed on board until the US Immigration had cleared the ship. We were entering the United States of America with a "green card," a permanent resident card for as long as we wished to stay. This is where we handed to the authorities our large envelope of x-rays and papers to enter the United States. Some people ignored the orders and missed a day of sightseeing to go to the hospital to have their X-rays taken and report back to the ship.

On shore, we hired a sea green, automatic Chevrolet Impala, which to us was huge. A couple, Bill and Diane Cawkell, returning to Canada offered to drive the car for us. We were glad as everything was backwards to driving in Australia. We were impressed with the lights at night on the hotels and nightclubs. Ironically, we were berthed near a Japanese warship.

Next day, we rose early, skipped breakfast and received beautiful leis on the dock from the Hawaiian women. We drove to Waikiki beach, Diamond Head, punchbowl cemetery, Pearl Harbor, and the Arizona Memorial. There was frangipani everywhere and smelled wonderful.

My first experience in the shops was a big surprise. I had selected some post cards and gave them the correct money only to find out they were charging me more than the price advertised for the cards. I didn't know that tax had to be added to the price. In Australia tax was always included in everything, including motorcars.

When we left Honolulu, a Hawaiian group wearing their native costumes joined our ship. They taught the children songs and dances. Their favorites were Little Brown Gal in a Little Grass Skirt, and Hukilau (a fishing throwing net). They sang those same songs for years.

Arriving in Los Angeles, USA

After five days at sea, we arrived in Los Angeles. We cleared customs and arranged for our crates to be sent by rail to St. Louis, Missouri.

Riots and unrest had started in America. We visited a Lutheran minister who had lived in L.A. for seven years and his home been robbed six times, usually when he went on vacation. One time, the robbers loaded all his furniture on a truck and stole it. We wondered if we had made a mistake by coming to a country with such unrest.

Jill, Michael, and Lisa loved the day we spent in Disney Land, Universal City Studios, Grauman Chinese Theatre, seeing the stars hand and footprints, and the Hollywood Bowl. It was a dream come true for all of us.

We left Los Angeles on a train to St. Louis. We sat in the dome car traveling through the Rockies enjoying the wonderful scenery. In those days, the passenger trains pulled over on a sidetrack to allow the freight trains to pass without stopping. We changed trains in Kansas City, but when we arrived, the train we were to board was already full with no seats for our family. We were temporarily asked to sit in the women's washroom for two hours while the porters located seats for us. Again, we wondered if we had made the right decision to come to America.

Norman Habel, who had arranged for Hubert to receive the call to Centralia, Illinois, met us at the Union Train Station in St. Louis. We stayed with Norm, Barbara, and their three children at the seminary for four days before driving us to Centralia, our new home.

Final Destination – A New Parish In Centralia, Illinois

It was the 2nd of July, 1968. The congregation members arranged to fully furnish the parsonage for our arrival. It was a wonderful surprise. The kitchen cabinets were filled with basic items and a meal was delivered to us at dinner time.

The first item of business was to purchase a car. A member who owned a car dealership suggested a used 1963 Chevrolet with 17,000 miles for $950 and $250 extra for air conditioning. It took a little while to get used to driving on the other side of the road.

Hubert was installed at 7 p.m. on Sunday, 7th July 1968. A large crowd with fifteen visiting clergy attended the evening service.

On Monday 8th July, the crates arrived and miraculously nothing was broken. We unpacked and settled into the house quite quickly. We were not used to central air conditioning and found it too cold in the house even on a hot day. But we soon got used to it. The children were given lots of toys including a bike for Michael. The neighbors children loved to listen to Jill, Michael, and Lisa with their strange accents.

Chapter 12

Our First American Homes

Centralia, Illinois – July 1968 – January 1977

Trinity Lutheran Church in Centralia, Illinois had over 1,000 church members and a school with 150 students from kindergarten through eighth grade. For Hubert, the routine is pretty much the same as it was in Australia: church services, many meetings, hospital visits, shut-ins, and home visits, only on a larger scale. He now had his office in the church complex, and for the first time had a full-time secretary, which he loved. She took care of all the mundane things that he used to do himself, and it freed him to do the more important aspects of his ministry. There were many large church denominations in this town of 30,000 people. The Sunday service was broadcast over the local radio station.

We were asked to speak about Australia on the radio show. There was much local interest about this new couple in town.

As far as we could see, there were corn fields (no fences) and oil wells, which is very common in Illinois and the Midwest. As the seasons were reversed from the Southern Hemisphere, we had to get used to the changes. Christmas was cold and often snowy.

The synodical church office of the Lutheran Church Missouri Synod is in St. Louis. There is a very large population of Lutherans living in the surrounding states. The Seminary is also in St. Louis where many of our Australian professors were guest lecturers for a year. It was great to see them when they came to visit us.

Most of the members of the congregation lived reasonably close to the church. Jill was in 6th grade, Michael in 3rd, and Lisa in kindergarten. They adjusted well to their new school and made many friends with whom they still stay in contact.

Grocery shopping was quite a challenge. All the food labels were different, and things I was used to buying were just not available; and there were no substitutes. The way I used to cook suddenly changed. The members helped me though and I learned to cook the American way. We loved the Jell-0 salads that were popular back then.

I was asked if I would like to be the principal's secretary in the morning while Lisa was in kindergarten. I accepted the challenge and was in charge of the mail, newsletters, daily announcements, fundraising events, etc. As we lived just two blocks from the school, it was easy for me to walk to work.

We left a Mediterranean climate and had no overcoats or snow boots for the cold snowy winter we were about to experience. When the first snow fell, the phone rang and I was asked if they could pick me up and take me to school. I thanked them but said, "No thanks, I would like to walk in the snow." I loved it.

A group of friends took us to St. Louis for our first baseball game. We didn't know which team we should "barrack" (cheer) for, but we soon found out in a very loud way. The St. Louis Gateway Arch opened in 1965 and is one of the world's tallest monument. It symbolizes the gateway to the west.

Halloween is very popular in America (something we had never heard of). The church and school parents decorated a float for the parade of floats and marching bands in the street. Lisa was asked to ride on the church float, which won first place. The children went from door to door saying, "Trick or Treat" and were given candy for their baskets. Other traditions were not always good as our house with many trees was "tee-peed" with toilet paper, and the screens on the windows were marked with candle wax. Empty boxes were piled high in the driveway just to see how the new minister and his family handled Halloween.

We had only been in Centralia three months when our family was attending a "Night with Pastor" at the church. When we returned home, we noticed the back door was wide open and the lock was broken. We were scared as we thought the robber might still be in the house. My opal jewelry and other treasures were gone. We were in shock to say the least. The police were notified, and several months later they found the thief, and most of my jewelry was safely returned.

As we had expected to leave America and return to Australia after a reasonable time, we wanted to see as much of America as we could. We bought a used travel trailer and set off each summer vacation to a different destination. We travelled as far as Quebec and saw all the other major cities in Eastern Canada, the St. Lawrence River, Niagara Falls, Washington DC, New York City and Philadelphia. The journey out west included Denver and Pike's Peak, the Badlands, the Black Hills, Mt. Rushmore, Yellowstone, Zion and Bryce national parks, Hoover Dam, Las Vegas, Salt Lake City and the Grand Canyon. The southern route included Dallas, New Orleans, Alligator Alley, Miami, Key West, Cape Canaveral, Kenney Space Center, Daytona Beach, the Great Smokey Mountains, Atlanta and back home to Centralia. It was more than most local people had ever seen, and folks were amazed we were so adventuresome. It was the Aussie in us.

We purchased a color TV and enjoyed the difference from black and white. It was easy to get used to an air-conditioned house and car, which we did not have in Australia.

Another new event was Thanksgiving Day. It started with a church service and then we were invited to a member's home for a wonderful turkey dinner. The first year, we watched the Rose Bowl Parade in California. The Lutheran Hour float won an award in their category. The design on the float was covered and stuffed with fresh or dried flowers by people called "petal pushers".

Hubert's father suddenly died in 1971 and Hubert returned to Australia for the funeral. The Centralia congregation arranged for a wreath to be sent for the funeral. Because flowers were cheaper in Australia, the wreath barely fit in the trunk of his brother-in-law's large Dodge car. The wreath was almost as tall as his five-foot mother.

The children became proficient in basketball, softball, baseball, cheerleading, water skiing, swimming, and ice skating on the frozen ponds in the wintertime. Jill continued with her ballet classes. Michael tried his skill at the "punt, pass, and kick" competition. He won the local, won the zone, and went to the state, but lost. Still a very good effort as he had never played with an American football. We continued to enjoy golf and win trophies occasionally.

Michael and Lisa started paper routes in the streets around us. They delivered the papers in the evening, and again on Sunday mornings. The people were very generous with tips when they collected the money for the papers. They were allowed to spend half and save the other half in their bank accounts. Jill earned her money babysitting and life-guarding at the country club pool.

In 1971, we were robbed again. This time by three delinquent school lads who knocked on doors in the neighborhood to see if anyone was home. They were looking for money but were caught when they became too bold, and handed over the goods they had stolen. This time we put more locks, chains, and a padlock on the doors.

We watched TV with great excitement when the American astronauts landed on the moon. What an achievement.

When Jill and Michael were in high school, they acted and sang in the annual plays. I searched the thrift stores for costumes, but ended up making the many outfits that were required for each musical. They were sometimes quite elaborate, and took many hours to sew sequins on some of the dresses.

An annual event for the high school was the May Fete when the King and Queen of the court were crowned. The dresses were gorgeous and all hand made.

We hosted and led tours to New Zealand and Australia. The folks loved the fact they were shown around these countries with an Aussie. It was my first trip back in five years, and loved seeing our families and friends again.

After over eight years in this Midwest town, Hubert received and accepted the call to Baltimore, Maryland. There were many farewells. The moving van was packed. Jill and Michael helped us drive the 800 miles. Unfortunately, it started to snow as we drove through the Pennsylvania Mountains and was still snowing when we arrived in Baltimore. Illinois was very flat and Maryland hilly. It was a nice change, but hard to negotiate the hills in the snow.

Baltimore, Maryland – January 1977 – June 1987

The President of the congregation met us at Immanuel Lutheran Church on the corner of Loch Raven & Belvedere to show us this beautiful gothic stone cathedral building. In 1951, the interior was awarded the best design in America. It has a large intricate carved reredos and a marble altar. The stained-glass windows, valued at over two million dollars, can be compared with those in European cathedrals. It had a 4,000-pipe organ in the front and another one in the balcony. I was privileged to sing with the forty-five-voice volunteer choir. It had a membership of 1,000 with 130 enrolled in the school from kindergarten through sixth grade. The organist Richard Wegner also taught sixth-grade in the school.

A lovely office, recently redecorated by the Ladies Guild, was where Hubert spent his time at the church. A secretary handled all the office duties for him.

The President then took us to our rented row home two blocks from the church. A row home is a narrow house attached to about twenty other homes the same size, with a small back yard, no garage, and an alley between the back of the row homes behind us. We parked on the street, and first come, first got the spaces. If you were very lucky, you got one in front of your house. We moved in with snow everywhere. We didn't see our back yard for six weeks until it started to melt.

Jill was finishing her second year at Carbondale University 50 miles from Centralia, Illinois, Michael was in his junior year, and Lisa in eighth grade at Baltimore Lutheran High School just five miles away.

After three months we were able to purchase our first home just down the street from the row home. Ironically it had been the former minister's home, but had changed hands before we arrived. It was a two-story home on a corner block.

A member who was president of the Baltimore Oriole Baseball team gave us four tickets and a car pass to every home game at Memorial Stadium; what a nice perk. In 1983 we saw the Orioles win the World Series.

The organist Richard Wegner and my husband produced, "Hymn's Triumphant," a symphonic choral suite based on forty-two traditional hymns centered around the Lord's Prayer. A small orchestra with strings, trumpets, and drums accompanied the choir. Dick Wegner was the conductor. The church was packed with extra seats in the aisles. It was so well received we repeated it the next year.

The congregation arranged a celebration for Hubert's twenty-five years in the ministry, and our twenty-fifth wedding anniversary. The members graciously invited us to their homes or treated us to restaurant dinners. They were very kind and loving to our family.

Just by accident, we met two Aussies, Croft and Diana Henry, who were living in New York City while Croft was working for Forbes Magazine. Malcolm Forbes' yacht was anchored in New York City. Croft was entertaining some business people and invited us to join them on one of those trips. We had an incredible time cruising around Manhattan eating delicious food and drinks. The yacht had a crew of 14.

The Inner Harbor in Baltimore was undergoing a transformation from the old wharfs and storage buildings to smart new shops and restaurants with outdoor seating for people to sit and watch the harbor boat traffic. It was a great tourist attraction. We took visitors there many times. Little Italy with lots of eating places was close by.

In 1812, Fort McHenry defended Baltimore from the attack by the British with their ships anchored in the Chesapeake Bay. When friends were in town, it was a favorite place to visit. I also drove to Washington D.C. and showed them the White House, the Capital Building,

Smithsonian buildings, Arlington National Cemetery, Ford's Theater, and other historic sites.

Again we led tours to New Zealand, Australia, Jordan, Israel, Egypt, and Greece.

Lisa came with us on our first visit to London. As a little girl, I always dreamed of seeing the Queen in the palace. We drove around England and fell in love with the country. We stayed in bed and breakfast houses and enjoyed the fresh fish and chips, pies and pasties. It was like eating food we loved from Australia.

Later we went back to England and Scotland with friends from Centralia. We saw lots of castles, cathedrals, St. Andrew's Golf Club, Edinburgh, Parliament House, changing of the guard at Buckingham Palace, Westminster Abbey, St. Paul's Cathedral, and the Tower of London. We were fortunate to see the Royal Family lay a wreath at Trafalgar Square on Armistice Day.

We loved going to the beach at Ocean City, Maryland whenever we could get away for a few days. We loved it when the surf was suitable for body surfing. We taught our children how to do it.

I worked as a secretary part- time for a handicapped school whose students were trained to work for public agencies. Their work was very rewarding and gained praise from their employers.

In 1983, we flew to Madrid, Spain, and started our journey back-packing around Europe. We purchased a Eurail pass and rode trains everywhere. Before we left the States, we had written to "Berto". Remember him from Australia when he was a POW and lived with us during the war and fire? We had written to him and arranged to see him when we visited Florence. He was married with a daughter who spoke English. His daughter picked us up at our guesthouse and drove us to Berto's mountain summer home where he greeted me by saying, "Welcome, Little June". I was just a young girl when he left Australia. Now I was married, with three children and was a grandmother. He remembered everything about the fire and his stay with us. He was thrilled to see me again. His wife spoke no English but busied herself preparing a lovely lunch. After all these years he still spoke English quite well.

We visited all the major cities in Italy, Monaco, Princess Grace and Prince Albert's palace, Monte Carlo, and took a train through the Swiss Alps with many tunnels through the mountains. We swam in the Rhine River as Europe was having a heat wave that summer. We often sat on the platforms of train stations eating the wonderful baked bread, sausage, and cheese with a bottle of wine (same price as a bottle of water).

We arrived in Frankfurt, Germany, to pick up Jill, Michael, and Lisa from the airport as they were joining us for a week touring Germany by car. We had so much fun driving along the Rhine visiting castles on the way, eating huge pretzels and drinking beer at the Hofbrauhaus in Munich. We stayed in Gasthauses, friendly family-owned homes. Hubert was able to converse with the little German he remembered from college days.

There is nothing better than Maryland crabs that come out of the Chesapeake Bay. Steamed crabs, crab cakes, imperial crab, sautéed crab and any other way they fix them is better than any place in the US. We often bought a bushel of crabs from a truck on the side of the road. I steamed them with beer and Old Bay seasoning, and ate them outside on our picnic table.

We were thrilled to have my parents visit us for Christmas. Many others came from Australia and Centralia. We loved showing them around.

An Update on the Children While We Lived in Baltimore, Maryland

Jill married a Centralia boy, Brad Sprehe, on 26th May 1979. They made their home in Centralia where she started her own ballet school teaching young girls different dance steps. The students showed off what they learned at the annual recitals. Jill and Brad had a son Kyle, a daughter Kristen, and another boy Kory. After a while she decided to go to St. Louis to train to become a Radiation Therapist. When she graduated, she was hired at Moffitt Cancer Center in Tampa as a Radiation Therapy Technologist where she is still working.

Michael joined the ROTC in his senior year at high school. He continued in the reserve while he went to Towson University. He graduated with a degree in sports management and a teaching degree. He taught in several schools before deciding to become a member of the Army National Guard. He graduated from Officer's Candidate school as a 2nd lieutenant and became a US Citizen. He returned to the Academy as an instructor to train new officers. Later, he was an assistant professor of military science at Western University in Maryland.

He became a Captain while in Maryland. He married Margaret (Maggie) Adams in Immanuel on the 9th January 1988. They had a daughter Anne.

Lisa finished high school and went to Pittsburg to attend a school which trained students for a career in the travel industry. She was hired as a reservationist for Air Florida in Miami. She received flying benefits, and we could fly "space available." It gave us many great trips in the States and overseas. She returned from Miami to work as a customer service agent for Piedmont at the Baltimore airport. Piedmont Airlines was sold to US Airways. In 1985 she was voted "agent of the month".

In 1988 Hubert received and accepted a call to become a Vice President of Development for the Wheat Ridge Foundation in Chicago. It was really hard to leave the many friends we had made in Baltimore, but it was time to go.

Chicago, Illinois – June 1988 – October 1991

Hubert (now shortened to Hu) became a Director of Individual Gifts for the Wheat Ridge Foundation. The office was in downtown Chicago on the corner of Michigan Avenue and Monroe Street facing Grant Park and Lake Michigan..

Wheat Ridge was a suburb of Denver where a Lutheran Tuberculosis Sanatorium was established in 1905. It closed when a cure for TB was discovered, but the foundation continued in Chicago. It's ministry of healing and service focuses on the support of short-term pilot, innovative, creative projects around the world in the broadly defined category of Christian healing. It is well known in Lutheran circles for their Christmas seals in raising money for their projects.

We purchased a condominium formerly owned by Tony Accardo (known as the "big tuna," drug lord for organized crime in Chicago). The condo had an underground parking garage with a heated ramp from the street into the garage to melt the ice and snow in the wintertime. We lived just around the corner from Concordia University where we attended many choir recitals, band concerts, and plays performed by the students at the University.

Hu rode the Lake Street L train line raised above the streets to go to work in downtown Chicago. It was bitterly cold in the winter with wind blowing off the lake. One year we actually saw the lake frozen.

The Sears Tower was the tallest building in the world when we were there, so it was a great place to take visitors for the long-distance views if the weather was clear. Sometimes we were so far above the clouds all we saw was the blue sky above us and beautiful cloud formations below as if the city didn't exist.

Hu's main purpose was to visit donors around the country. We lived 20 minutes from O'Hare, one of the busiest airports in the country. Because I had the privilege of flying stand-by, courtesy of Lisa's flying benefits with US Airways, I was often able to join him on many of his trips. Often, he was asked to preach on Sundays, which he loved, as he was not a parish pastor at this time.

An exciting event was in 1988 on Reformation Day when Paul Manz, an organist and composer of church music, played the organ in Orchestra Hall accompanied by the Chicago symphony orchestra.

The annual, *Taste of Chicago,* held in Grant Park gave us a chance to sample foods from restaurants around the city. In the summer, the Symphony Orchestra performed free concerts from the sound shell in Grant Park. We often took a picnic supper with a bottle of wine to these very popular concerts. A fund-raiser for Wheat Ridge was at the Planetarium where the skies were designed to look like the Bethlehem skies with the "Star of Wonder."

We loved living in Chicago but hated the cold, snow, and blustery windy weather when the winters seemed so long. Because of our previous travels and the ones with Wheat Ridge, we have now visited every state in the USA.

I was the baby sitter for Jill's three children in Tampa for three weeks while Jill and Brad visited our family and friends in Australia. It had been a long time since I had sole charge of young children. We all survived, and I was able to turn them back to their parents safe and sound when Jill and Brad returned to the States.

Jill and her family remained in Tampa, Florida. Michael moved to Jacksonville, Arkansas where there is a large Air Force base and the headquarters for the Army National Guard where he was a professional education instructor. Their son Andrew was born on Armistice Day, 11th November 1990. My husband baptized Andrew in Baltimore on our 35th wedding anniversary on 30th December 1990. Lisa bought a condominium in Baltimore closer to the airport for her work. I flew back to help her decide where to live and with decorating, etc.

I was in Adelaide to surprise my parents for their 60th wedding anniversary when Hu called me to say he had received an invitation out of the blue. We were to fly to Hong Kong in two-weeks-time for Hu to be considered as a candidate to be the minister at the Church of All Nations in Repulse Bay. In just two weeks, I was crossing the Pacific Ocean twice. My jet lag couldn't catch up with me. We were the last of the candidates to be considered for the position. It was a whirlwind with officials of the church showing us around this exciting city, attending meetings, and learning what would be expected of us. We returned home in a daze. It had all happened so quickly.

Hong Kong made their decision and decided to call Hu to be their new pastor.

Our exciting life now became even more exciting as we headed to China for the challenge before us.

Chapter 13

Hong Kong, China
October 1991 – June 1996

It was quite hectic as we prepared to cross the Pacific once again. I was a very exciting time as Hu accepted the call to be the pastor of the Church of All Nations in Repulse Bay, Hong Kong Island. Living in a foreign country was not something we had expected, but we were looking forward to the challenge. Our church was mostly for English speaking ex-patriots from different countries. A great organist and choir enhanced the worship service. There were about 25 Philippine amahs (domestic maids) worshipping with us. Once a month, they sang Christian songs in their native Tagalog instead of the church choir. We enjoyed the change of pace and their lovely singing. Sunday mornings were a high point as there were always many international visitors attending the service.

Clergy from the USA, Australia, India, South Africa, the Philippines, Korea, and Hong Kong attended the installation. It was the third country where my husband had been installed as a parish pastor. In the summer, the congregation constantly changes as business people typically only stay three years in a foreign country. Teachers sign a contract for three years, but that can be extended.

A Chinese Christian artist attended our church services. He spoke a little English and wanted to contribute to the church budget but didn't know how. A member working at Kodak offered to print his artistry for Christmas cards that could be sold to the members. It worked wonderfully. He lived in a small shack below our home in Shouson Hill. He painted on the floor where he and his wife slept. A small stove for cooking and bathroom were in the corner. He showed us his paintings and we arranged to take them to the church for a display after the service. He received many offers to paint for our members. He was on his way to becoming famous. After we left Hong Kong, he rented a studio in the city and became well known in wider circles. We were happy the members helped him achieve his dream. The Chinese often use gold leaf in their picture framing. Some of his paintings now hang in our Florida home.

The Hong Kong International School from K – 12th grade is the largest school in the Lutheran Church Missouri Synod. There are two campuses, one for K – 6th grade in Repulse Bay, and from 7th-12th in Tai Tam, the far end of the Island. All children must speak English to attend, even the fifty percent of Chinese who live in Hong Kong or come from the People's Republic of China. They chose our school for their children as it was a stepping stone to the Universities in America. There are about 350 educators and staff from many different countries, many with university degrees. I was asked to be a part-time "para" (a teacher's aide). I worked, when I was available, with K-2nd grade. I loved working with the little ones. I was asked to help ex-pat wives look for housing, how to use the public transportation system, shopping and finding suitable schools for their children.

The Chinese government asked our church officials if they would start a sister school in Shanghai for the expats living there. It became an extremely successful school and still is today.

According to the airline pilots, Kai Tak airport on Kowloon is the most challenging approach to a runway in the world. They head straight for the big red and white checkerboard on the mountain, make a sharp right turn, fly low over the roof tops of the houses, and drop sharply to the runway below between the mountain and the harbor. Fortunately, the pilot told us what was about to happen, but it was still incredibly scary the first time. When Lisa came to visit us the first time, the plane was about to land in a typhoon (hurricane) but was diverted to the Philippines as a plane before couldn't stop in time and ended in the water at the end of the runway.

While the parsonage was being painted, and the beautiful teak floors sanded and stained, we lived for four weeks on the fourth floor (no lift) in an apartment owned by the school in Stanley Market. It overlooked the outdoor eating houses, all kinds of clothing and linen shops, jewelry and Chinese souvenir stores. Very early in the morning, around 5 am, the market came alive as the delivery trucks rolled in banging the truck doors and speaking loudly in Chinese. Sleep was impossible after that rumpus.

The parsonage was a flat on the third floor (no lift) of a building in Shouson Hill. The flat roof was ours, and we made good use of it. We often entertained visitors there, and when I cooked lamb on the grill they referred to it as "a rooftop experience." We had a great view of

Aberdeen and the water in the distance. We could see the traffic entering the tunnel to take them into the city.

When the ex-pats left to return to their own countries, they were eager to sell some furniture they weren't taking with them. This supplemented what we needed to make our home more comfortable. We often received "dragon pots" with lovely plants for the roof top garden.

Shopping was a challenge. When I was preparing for visitors, I had my list ready for the grocery store only to find they were out of the main ingredient. When I asked when they would have it, the manager said, "Boat no bring – maybe next week." I stood in the store and mentally changed my whole menu for the food that was available. It was a culture shock, as few Chinese spoke English, but somehow we managed to communicate to let them know what we wanted.

Learning to convert American dollars to Hong Kong dollars took a little time. I seemed to have so much money in my purse, but really I didn't. 100 HK dollars was just over 7 American dollars.

I learned to drive in the busy, horn-honking, snarled traffic. Sometimes it took twenty minutes to go to the airport through the tunnel to the Kowloon side, and sometimes an hour. You just never knew and had to plan accordingly. We drove to the Chinese border (Peoples Republic of China) through the mountains, rice paddy fields, markets, and high rise buildings that were not there twenty five years ago when we stopped there on our way to America. The Hakka ladies try to sell you things and won't leave you alone until you buy a post card from them.

We experienced five or six typhoons that are called hurricanes in America. One was particularly bad. When the wind is higher than forty miles an hour, all public transport stops. The heavy rain causes mudslides down the mountains, uprooting trees and blocking the roads. On one occasion, an apartment building on the top of a mountain tumbled down killing many people.

When the American fleet anchored in the south China Sea, including an aircraft carrier and other ships of the fleet, came to Hong Kong, we were invited to attend a reception on the carrier with good American food and a champagne fountain. We were treated on the flight deck to a "silent drill team" performance. It was very impressive.

The sailors loved it when they were in port for Thanksgiving, because our church invited as many as we could to join us for an American Thanksgiving dinner with all the trimmings. One year we invited the navy choir to sing for our Christmas Eve service. This is why Hong Kong is so exciting when unexpected things like that happen.

Hu had the incredible experience of leaving Kai Tak airport on the Navy mail plane to fly 200 miles into the South China Sea and landing on the deck of the USS Kitty Hawk. He spent the day watching the planes takeoff and land on the deck. The most dangerous job in the world is working on the deck of a carrier. At the end of the day they catapulted off the aircraft for their return to Hong Kong.

Each time you fly out of Hong Kong, you are going on an International flight and your passport gets stamped every time, quickly filling the pages. Fortunately, we were able to add more pages when we renewed our passports. We left Hong Kong in the summer vacation to return to the US to see our children and grandchildren. Many of the ex-pats, teachers, and other workers did the same. The planes were always packed. It was a fifteen-hour flight to the west coast. If there are head winds on the return trip, the planes were diverted to Taiwan to refuel. It made the journey so much longer.

In March 1994, I returned to help Lisa plan her wedding which was to be in August that year. It was fun shopping for a wedding dress and veil, choosing my dress, selecting a venue for the reception, and all the things that are needed for a smooth event. She married Greg Schaub in the Immanuel Lutheran Church in Baltimore on 20th August 1994. It was the first time in five years our family had been together.

We loved to show Hong Kong to Jill and Brad from Tampa, Michael and Maggie from Hawaii, and Lisa and Greg from Baltimore when they came to visit us. Many family and friends from Australia came to see us also. We were constantly entertaining church officials and friends from America.

In 1995, I was preparing to leave Hong Kong and fly to Hawaii to visit Michael and his family. I woke up at 4 am and entered the small office where we had a TV. I glanced in the room, with a little light from the moon and saw a Chinese man crouched in the corner. I screamed and made a quick retreat to our bedroom where Hu was being rudely awakened by my screaming. With all my might, I quickly pulled the dresser across in front of the door as it didn't have a lock. We wanted to call the police and we knew it wasn't 911, but couldn't remember the right one. Finally we managed to call them and they arrived quite promptly. I wasn't about to leave the bedroom in case the robber was still in the house. I sang out of the bathroom window to the police below, and said I would throw the keys to them and they could let themselves into the building and our apartment. They searched every room but found no one. We found the casement window in the office wide open. We left the window open just a little in case it rained during the night, as we had no central air conditioning. As the Chinese are very agile, the robber had climbed up the drainpipe to the third floor, and entered the room. He took all the cash we had as I had just been to the bank the day before. My one thought as he left the room, probably in a big hurry, maybe he hurt his leg on the way down. Fortunately, I stopped him before he went into the rest of the house or even our bedroom, as they were sometimes known to harm the residents.

An unusual sight was the densely populated "Walled City" in Kowloon. There were hovels one right next to the other with small passages like a rabbit warren running through them. Chinese troops were forced to vacate the area which had become a safe haven for criminals, prostitutes, gangs, and drug lords hidden in a network of dark alleys. It was leveled in 1993 and transformed into a park.

Shortly after we arrived, the members of the church council decided the kitchen needed a renovation. It was gutted, and new cabinets were ordered from Germany. I couldn't use the kitchen for two months, which meant the council arranged for us to eat our evening meals at members' homes. A nice treat.

The famous Jumbo Floating Restaurant in Aberdeen is in the style of a Chinese Imperial Palace. It was reached by taking a ferryboat or a "san pan." It had many dining rooms and served hundreds of people. You could choose your own fish from the fish tanks on the back of the boat. They entertained Queen Elizabeth and many famous actors.

A cable vehicular tram takes you to the Peak where on a clear day the views overlooking Hong Kong and the harbor are spectacular, or you may even see a plane make a precarious landing in Kia Tak. The view of the lights at night is something you must see.

The Star Ferry crosses the harbor every few minutes from Hong Kong Island to Kowloon. It is cheap, crowded, and fun. When you learn how to utilize the well-operated underground train system, it will take you very quickly to your destination.

The Hong Kong Philharmonic Orchestra is well known throughout the world. Many famous artists are engaged to perform in the orchestra hall across the harbor. We enjoyed their concerts.

I climbed the mountain trails to see the spectacular views of Hong Kong from every advantage point. It was rugged, and sometimes the trails were non-existent, but my friends and I enjoyed it so much. To keep in shape, we played tennis on the school courts whenever time permitted. When Lisa came to visit, we walked everywhere, faster than she wanted, and she said "Mum,

I want to see Hong Kong with you, not from behind you."

We watched the dragon boat races in Stanley and the many street parades featuring the dragons with bright colors and a massive head dancing around with drums and cymbals clanging.

Christmas is always a special time and Hong Kong was no exception. Driving around the city to see the lights at night is not to be missed. To do just that, our friends, Anita and Dave, rented a double decker bus with an open top. People of the streets stopped to watch the bus as we drove by singing Christmas carols with lots of enthusiasm.

Chinese New Year is not to be outdone with their incredible lights surpassing even the great displays at Christmas. This is their most impressive festival.

There are hundreds of islands around Hong Kong, many of which are uninhabitable.

Lamma Island is well known for serving seafood and particularly "peppered prawns." It takes about half-an-hour by ferry boat, junk or san pan, but it is worth it.

Lantau Island is quite a bit larger and a bus ride takes you to the Buddhist Monastery where you can climb many steps to the top to see the huge Buddha with outstretched arms.

Macau, then owned by Portugal, has many Chinese antique shops that are sought after by Hong Kong residents and tourists. A high-speed hovercraft gets you there very quickly. There are several gambling casinos if that is your thing.

June Temme
Beijing, China

Once a month, the minister living in Hong Kong, who spoke fluent Mandarin, went to China to check on the American teachers working in small groups teaching English to the Chinese. We accompanied him on our first time to China visiting Beijing, Shanghai, and Hangzhou. It was a great experience to climb the Great Wall, visit Tiananmen Square, the Forbidden City, and in Shanghai we walked along the Bundt where the financial offices are located and visited a tea garden. Before we left Hong Kong, I had climbed the Great Wall three times including a large part of the unrestored wall, which proved to be very strenuous. My muscles hurt for days.

In Hangzhou, we attended a Chinese church service with 1,500 people in attendance. They seated us in the front row, and we listened to the forty-minute sermon in Chinese. Our friend whispered in our ear to let us know what he was talking about. As the congregation spilled out onto the street after the service; there were no police around to stop the people worshipping in a Christian church. After all, it was a communist country where Christianity was not allowed. After the service it was interesting to meet the ministers who had been under house-arrest during the Cultural Revolution.

My husband was asked to preach once a month in Beijing for the State Department Embassy staff who came from around the world. The service was held in a hotel room and about twenty people attended. He presided over the funeral of a State Department official, and seated in the front row was a Secretary of the Communist Party. As a Christian minister, he was able to share the good news of the resurrection of Jesus Christ. Another example of being "Led by the Lord."

With the enthusiasm of the people, they formed a church called "The Congregation of the Good Shepherd." A permanent minister was called from South Africa. They gave us a fond farewell when we left Beijing. The congregation is still meeting to this day.

In 1996, my husband decided he would retire from active parish life and return to the States to be nearer our children.

We were overwhelmed with many farewell parties arranged by our friends as we prepared to leave this exciting city.

The Consul General of the American Embassy invited about fifty people for a dinner at his home on the Peak. Views were spectacular. Their staff served us a delicious meal. The chairwoman of the school board arranged a lovely dinner party for 20 people at her home. Another friend held a party at his home in Parkview Towers overlooking the city lights. A junk ride around the harbor with a dinner at a Chinese Restaurant was among the great times we had saying goodbye to our many friends in this International city.

Chapter 14

Countries We Visited During Our Stay In Hong Kong

As we were members of the International Asian Ministers Conference, we visited a different country for meetings each year. Our meetings consisted of a church service, bible study, fellowship, sharing, meeting new people, and visiting the local sites. We were pleased to see many Asian countries served by Lutheran pastors.

BANGKOK AND CHIANG MAI IN THAILAND

Bangkok has many beautiful temples with lots of gold were everywhere. The Tuk Tuk primitive, smelly gas cars, drove us around. The city is crowded, hot and humid and not very clean.

Chiang Mai is where we attended our first International Asian Ministers Conference. We met the ministers and their wives from different denominations. We rode an elephant, visited a Leper Colony, a Christian home for young girls rescued from rampart prostitution, and saw many handmade craft markets.

KUALA LUMPUR, MALAYSIA

We visited the Batu Caves, the most popular holy shrines for a Hindu festival in Malaysia. There are 272 steps leading into the cave. The monkeys living in the cave may pose a biting hazard for tourists as they can be quite territorial.

SEOUL, SOUTH KOREA

A highlight was attending the largest Christian church in all Christendom with 770 pastors, 750,000 members and 23,000 worshippers at each of the six services on a Sunday. Ushers directed our group to a special place in the church where we were given head phones to listen to the service in English. They even sang the same tune we know for the Lord's Prayer and the Apostles Creed. An organ, orchestra, and choir accompanies the congregational singing. A bus took us to the Demilitarized Zone at Panmunjom at the North Korean border. The building is unusual. If you stand on one side of the table you are in South Korea and on the other side you are in North Korea with the respective guards outside the window. The massive loud speakers send propaganda for miles around by the North Korean communist government.

SINGAPORE, MALAYA

Singapore is probably the cleanest city in the world. They are very strict about littering, etc. During WW11, the Japanese occupied Singapore from 1942-1945. Singapore was officially returned to British colonial rule on 12th September 1945 following a formal signing of the surrender.

BALI

We saw duck farms, local farmers, and villages as we drove in the countryside with friends from Hong Kong. The conference was held in a hotel on the beach with many shops close by selling local wares where you could bargain with the merchants.

GUAM, US TERRITORY

Hu was asked to lead a weekend retreat for the International Lutherans living in Guam. The minister of the congregation is also the chaplain for the Air Force base.

It was interesting to see the island as the Americans fought a bitter battle against the Japanese to keep the island in American hands. There was a strong earthquake that rocked the island and destroyed many lovely nativity sets among other things in the chaplains home.

MANILA, PHILIPPINES

We enjoyed visiting Manila again, as we were there on our cruise to America. It hadn't changed and the city was still dirty. An interesting thing happened on our return flight to Hong Kong. We were waiting in the 1st class lounge when the last British Governor of Hong Kong, Chris Patton, walked in and sat down to talk to us. He asked Hu, "What is your bible text for Sunday morning?" A very interesting question. Our picture was taken with him and his wife, and he said he would sign it when I had it printed. A nice gesture. They were met in Hong Kong with security guards and we followed behind them through the airport. The British Governor was in Hong Kong to oversee the handover of Hong Kong to China in 1997.

TOKYO, JAPAN

We stayed with the Lutheran Minister in Tokyo for two days before the conference when Hu preached for the Sunday service. It is a bustling city with everyone talking on cell phones and not looking where they are walking. We met a famous Christian Japanese artist who spoke at our conference. He loved to paint bible stories.

TAIPEI, TAIWAN

We attended the annual meeting of the board of the Christian Salvation Service in Taipei of which Hu is a member. They operate a baby rescue clinic for babies born with birth defects and not tolerated by the Chinese. Americans fly to Taiwan and readily adopt them.

Chang Kai-Shek the Chinese military and political leader was defeated and exiled in 1949 by Mao Zedong, the new leader of the Peoples Republic of China. Chang fled to Taiwan and smuggled large quantities of gold from China. The National Palace Museum is filled with antique porcelain and snuff bottles stolen from China. Many soldiers and civilians followed Chang to Taiwan.

HO CHI MONH CITY (SAIGON) VIETNAM

An unexpected invitation came for us to visit some Australian friends in Saigon. They lent us their car and driver to take us to the Cu Chi Tunnels. The Communist guerrilla troops known as the Viet Cong (VC) dug tens of thousands of miles of network tunnels. Soldiers used these underground routes to house troops, supplies and lay booby traps. We climbed down into the tunnels where there was a kitchen, hospital, and sleeping quarters. It was easy to see why the Americans couldn't win the war with this kind of warfare. The enemy were so cunning. If a bomb fell on one section of the tunnel they quickly dug around the crater. We toured the building where the last Americans were picked up by helicopters and flown to the waiting ships in the open water.

The markets were filled with beautiful hand-made table cloths and linens. Painted lacquered dishes and plates were popular with the tourists.

SRI LANKA and NEW DELHI, INDIA

On our flight to India, we landed at Colombo, the capital of Sri Lanka (formerly Ceylon). The Lutheran Missionary in Colombo was kind enough to take us with him when he went on his regular rounds visiting small Lutheran mission churches on the island. When we stopped for a cup of Ceylon tea, Hu was game enough to put a twenty-foot python around his neck while a cobra popped its head out of a basket.

We climbed the 1,200 steps to the top of a magnificent fortress at Sigiriya built in the 6th century. As we drove through the tea plantations, we were thinking of Hu's favorite movie, "Elephant Walk," as we watched the tea pickers. Our guide spoke seven different languages and showed us around the tea factory using the same kind of tea chests we used in Yalata for aboriginal baptisms, etc. This estate has 2,000 workers and a Lutheran church in the center of the plantations. Sri Lanka is known for their sapphires and rubies.

We left Sri Lanka to fly to New Delhi, India where we encountered much poverty, pollution, and beggars.

There are many rich people there as well. We visited some rug shops and purchased some beautiful Persian rugs, especially "priced" for us. They remind us of our trip to India and now grace our home in New Port Richey, Florida. We were warned not to eat or drink the food, so I took crackers, vegemite, bars, and cookies from Hong Kong. We only drank bottled water. For that reason we refused the lunch on the train to Agra. We used bacterial soap and wet wipes constantly and did not get sick as many tourists do. A hired car with driver and guide took us to Jaipur where we stayed in a Maharajah's palace. After dinner, we sat around the fire pit in the courtyard chatting with the Prince. The Taj Mahal with its white marble and semi-precious stones glistens in the sunlight. It was hard to leave such a beautiful place. It was dark when we drove back to New Delhi, but the drivers do not use their headlights. We were so scared we would crash into a bus with people sitting on the roof or hanging out the windows, camel and donkey wagons, or ox carts and motorbikes. An awful thought crossed our minds that we could die on a road in India and no one would know where we were. It was however, a trip to remember.

Chapter 15

Settling in New Port Richey, Florida

We left Hong Kong and flew to Australia to celebrate the 50th anniversary of Concordia College in Toowoomba where Hu was in the original class and his father was the Principal. Next stop was Adelaide to celebrate the 40th anniversary of Hu's graduation from Concordia Seminary. We said goodbye to family again, and flew to Hawaii where Michael lived with Maggie, Anne, Andrew, and Joey who was born on October 2, 1995. Then we made a quick visit to Baltimore to see Lisa and Greg and finally on to Tampa, Florida.

It was hard to leave Hong Kong and think about retirement. Not quite so fast. When our daughter Jill found out we were returning to the States, she said the Lutheran minister at her church in Temple Terrace, Florida told her he could use some help and offered Hu a part time job. Hu helped with the parish visiting, preached about once a month, and took a turn teaching bible study. So, we started looking for a place to live. Jill, Brad, Kyle, Kristen, and Kory live near the church so we were able to see them every Sunday. An interesting side note, we soon found out that Tampa is the "lightning capital of the world."

After living in Hong Kong, we didn't want to live in the cold and snow any more. We settled on Timber Greens, in New Port Richey, which is a town on the gulf coast of Florida about 40 miles from Tampa. It is a deed-restricted community with a golf course that requires residents to be 55 or older. The gated community with 800 homes was reasonably close to the airport and beach. It sounded ideal to us; it was, and still is. The community was just getting started back then. Building blocks were available, there were no paved streets or sidewalks, and the clubhouse and golf course were still being completed. A lovely big pool with a hot tub, tennis courts, and a bocce ball court are now next to the clubhouse. Most people who live here own their own golf cart, so we followed suit and we purchased a used golf cart hoping to play lots of golf. We both loved playing golf and enjoy seeing the wild life such as wild turkeys, peacocks, otters, alligators, and armadillos who dig big holes in the garden, egrets, sand hill cranes, and deer who munch on flowers in the front garden.

Our belongings were scattered all over the country when we left for Hong Kong. The boxes came from everywhere and even my goods that had been stored at my parent's home were shipped to Florida. It was like Christmas seeing what I had left behind.

Ministerial Life in Florida

My husband started the tradition of an Easter sunrise service on the eleventh fairway of our golf course. We watched the sun rise over the lake and trees while the people sat in their golf carts or chairs in a semi-circle surrounding the lectern. Later, our church Praise Band and singers provided the music for the service. It is still popular with the community with often over 200 worshippers attending.

The President of the Florida-Georgia District of the Lutheran Church asked Hu if he would go to Nassau in the Bahamas, as the church needed a vacancy pastor. We went for a week once a month and that lasted for eighteen months as well as the Temple Terrace ministry. In Nassau, we stayed in the parsonage, found our way around the island, and conducted regular parish duties. It didn't take too long for us to enjoy the Bahamian conch fritters. The congregation is mostly black Bahamian and the ladies call me "honey child," a term of endearment.

A nice surprise, one Sunday at church was to meet a member of a TV show, "The Little Rascals." He was quite old when we talked with him but he remembered how he rode in the wagon going very fast down hill when it tipped over and he fell out.

We attended an Intentional Interim training seminar in Florida, and at the conclusion, Hu was asked to go to Mt. Olive Lutheran Church in Newton, North Carolina to help heal the congregation after an unpleasant situation had occurred. We stayed for six months and made many friends. The area was famous for the woolen mills and furniture makers.

Another congregation experiencing a crisis was in Nags Head, North Carolina. I enjoyed climbing all the lighthouses along the coast. We drove along the Outer Banks, visited Kitty Hawk where the Wright Brothers flew their first plane, and attended a play on Roanoke Island where the new British Colony disappeared without a trace.

We also spent six weeks healing the rift in the congregation in El Paso, Texas. It was good to see our friends Tim and Kathie from Baltimore, now living in El Paso. Interstate 10 runs through the center of the city, and on the mountain if you look up while driving at night, you see a lighted cross. On Easter Sunday night it was lit in our honor by the members of Zion Lutheran Church in recognition and appreciation for helping them in time of need.

Dr. Dale Meyer, the President of Concordia Seminary, St. Louis, Missouri, asked Hu to be a deployed Regional Director of Development in Florida working from our home in New Port Richey. I accompanied Hu around Florida where we visited and met many donors, many of whom we have remained friends with over the years. We attended regular meetings in St. Louis and often stopped to visit friends in Centralia, Illinois, our first parish in America.

Hu was the recipient of an honorary Doctorate of Divinity from Concordia Seminary, St. Louis, Missouri, on 20th May 2011. Our three children and five of our ten grandchildren attended this momentous occasion. It was held in the chapel of St. Timothy and St. Titus during the commencement exercises for the graduates entering the ministry. Dr. Meyer presented him with a diploma, cap, gown, and stole. It is an honor Rev. Dr. Hubert Temme and his family will never forget.

A Lutheran church was formed in Georgetown, Grand Cayman Island, and retired ministers were asked to spend two or three weeks preaching to the islanders and visiting tourists. We spent nine years helping them out in the summer. We met on Sundays in a room provided by a hotel. I loved snorkeling and seeing the most amazing fish in every part of the island. I also loved swimming with the stingrays as they came right up to me while I stood waist deep on a sand bar. They took fish from my outstretched hand. Unfortunately, Hurricane Ivan, with winds of 220 mph, almost devastated the island. Caskets were floating in the cemeteries, cars piled five high on top of each other, ferry boats ended up in the hotel parking lot, fish were displaced, roads were impassible, and turtles from the turtle farm washed out to sea. Except for Georgetown, there was no electricity on the island. Six feet of water came through the streets where the parsonage was, destroying it. Every home had major damage. We were asked to go back to offer the members counseling and healing for them and the members of the island. We cooked on a small camp gas stove and showered in cold water, living much like we did on our camping excursions in Australia. Swimming pools were filled with sand. 95% of all buildings were damaged. No cruise ships were able to take tourists to the island for months until it was repaired. It was a sad return to this former vibrant place in the Caribbean.

We spent two weeks in Wittenberg, Germany, where Hu served as a summer minister preaching in the Castle Church where Martin Luther nailed the 95 thesis, and preached in the Stadtkirche where Martin Luther himself preached for over thirty years. This was a high point for Hu and his ministry.

While Michael was spending three years on an Army base in Stuttgart, Germany, Hu preached many times at the base Lutheran Chapel. Michael's son Andrew was confirmed together with other Army children in Worms, Germany. Hu was privileged to be the preacher and confirm the children.

During a vacancy in Immanuel Lutheran Church, Baltimore, the congregation asked my husband to help them out for a few months. It was good to see our old friends, listening to the great organ music, and worship in that great church again.

Friends from Hong Kong asked Hu to conduct a sunset wedding on a catamaran out of Key West, another a wedding in Fort Wayne, Indiana, and then a special birthday and wedding in San Francisco. We loved seeing our friends again for their special events.

After forty years in the active ministry and no longer in a parish, we were able to visit our children in Tampa or Virginia for Christmas and other special holidays.

On the Lighter Side

Hong Kong friends who worked at the US State Department invited us to their home in Pretoria, South Africa, where they had been transferred. They arranged for a guide to take us to Kruger National Park for four days. From early morning to dusk, we drove slowly through the reserve looking for animals. We were fortunate to see the "big five," lions, elephants, leopards, rhinoceros, and the Cape buffalo, plus giraffes, hippopotamus, zebra, deer, monkeys, etc. We stayed in cottages inside a compound protected by armed guards and an electric fence to separate us from the wild animals that roamed and roared at night. We toured Cape Town, rounded the Cape of Good Hope, saw many vineyards, Robben Island where Mandella was imprisoned, the imposing Table Mountain, and the Lutheran church which has been there for two centuries.

When my father died suddenly at age 94 years, I made a hurried trip to Adelaide to be with my mother and sisters. It was a nail-biting time as I was stuck in Denver because of snow and then landed in San Francisco in fog and wasn't sure I would make the flight to Australia. My mother died at age 93. They were married for 67 years.

We flew back again to Queensland to celebrate the great occasion of Hu's mother's 100th birthday. She wrote and memorized her speech. Until her later years she played the organ and decorated the flowers for the chapel services where she was residing in an assisted living home. She was an incredible lady and died before her 101st birthday. She lived in three centuries.

We enjoyed our first cruise so much that we continued this mode of travel for many years to see places we had always dreamed about visiting. One memorable cruise was flying to London, boarding a ship in Dover, going through the Kiel Canal, visiting Berlin, St. Petersburg, Helsinki, Stockholm, Copenhagen, and Oslo. On Hu's bucket list was an Atlantic crossing seeing the Canary Islands, Gibraltar, and ending in Rome. At different times we enjoyed a Mediterranean cruise starting in Rome, driving along the Amalfi coast in Italy, going to several Greek Islands, parts of the old unearthed city of Ephesus, Istanbul and ended in Venice. Other trips were to Reykjavik, Iceland a volcanic rock island, a river cruise in Portugal, the Panama Canal, Alaska catching and eating salmon, Eastern & Western Caribbean on the largest sailing ship in the world. In South America, starting our cruise in Valparaiso, we saw the magnificent glaziers along Chili, rounding Cape Horn, the Antarctic in the distance, stopping at the British Falkland Islands, and ending in Buenos Aires in Argentina.

We also had a wonderful trip to Warsaw, Poland, Auschwitz, Bucharest, Budapest, Hungry, Vienna, and Prague.

Other memorable places were two weeks with friends in Freiburg, Germany and again in Kauai, Hawaiian Islands. When Michael and Maggie were living in Stuttgart, Germany, we went with them to Ireland for our 50th wedding anniversary. We visited our dear friends Anita & Dave when they were living in Edinburgh, Scotland for a short time and drove around Scotland staying in Bed and Breakfast houses. We attended the famous "Military Tattoo" with marching bands from around the world playing bagpipes and drums in Edinburgh Castle.

While in Germany, travelling with friends, we stopped in Bellesen where my husband's family lived before migrating to Australia. We saw the church where his great grandfather was baptized and worshipped, the cemetery where family members are buried, the family home, and a monument in a small park with the name Temme on it.

Visiting the Christmas markets around Germany is like being in another world. Snow on the ground, it was freezing cold, and we wore hats, coats, and gloves to keep warm. It was our first time to enjoy eating German brats and drinking hot "Gluhwein" in special mugs . The markets were filled with hand-made wooden nativity sets, mangers, nutcrackers, knitted articles, needlework, cross stitching, tapestries, etc.

I was able to visit the town near Dresden where my mother's fore fathers lived. I climbed into the attic to see where the big bells hung to summon the worshippers to church on Sundays.

While in Germany, Michael took us to Poland to buy Polish pottery from the small family-owned home businesses scattered in small towns just over the German border. The pottery is beautifully hand-decorated and, when we were there, very reasonably priced. The pottery is oven-proof and microwavable safe. Buses with American military wives and tourists go to Poland every day as it is much more expensive to buy these same things in Germany and America.

One of the most exciting overseas trips was in 2003 when I returned to my hometown in Australia to celebrate its 150th anniversary of St. Michael's Lutheran Church in Tarrington, Victoria. I represented my family by attending the festivities and church service. Many friends from school that I hadn't seen since I left Tarrington were there, and we enjoyed swapping notes on family, what we were doing, and where we were living. We stayed in my farm home with my friends who had bought the farm from my father. It was good to see the place again and remember the good times I had there. The garden my mother loved so much was immaculate and fully recovered from that horrible fire day.

When we returned home, another exciting event was to meet Ken Ham, an Australian Christian man and a friend of ours who had a biblical vision. He had built the Creation Museum In Kentucky some years prior and with that success built a replica of Noah's Ark to biblical dimensions near Williamstown, Kentucky. Each year it attracts over 100,000 people, both Christian and non-believers. We are blessed to support this ministry and were guests at the ribbon cutting ceremony.

I must not forget to mention that during our retirement in Florida we experienced six hurricanes with trees down on the golf course, and one tree landed on the edge of our roof but there was no major damage to our community. We were so fortunate as the damage was nothing compared to what the Cayman Islands experienced.

Our 60th wedding anniversary was celebrated on 30th December 2015 with our three children, their spouses, 10 grandchildren (and two of their spouses), and 3 great grandchildren who attended our week of celebrations in New Port Richey. My sister Elizabeth, who was my flower girl at our wedding, came to be with us. Jill and Lisa helped with the decorations. We made our wine, Australian Shiraz, which was labeled, "established in 1955 and aged 60 years," with our picture on the front. Each guest received a bottle to take home. A friend made the two-tier anniversary cake from a picture of the original wedding cake and used the original cake topper which I had saved. Because it was so mild that year, the family was able to spend time in the pool to relax before the fun began. After the family dinner at the club house, our children and grandchildren decorated our golf cart with balloons and streamers, wrote on the window, and tied beer cans with long strings to the back of the cart. The great grandsons loved the ride home with us.

One summer, our friends, Pam and Fred from Seminole, took us on their boat to catch scallops in the Gulf. We managed to fill a bucket, but when they were taken out of the shell, we only had a small bowl of the meat, just enough for dinner. We needed to wear heavy gloves as the scallops can quickly nip your fingers. It was a new experience for us as the scallops hide in the shallow water hidden by grass.

Four times we attended the practice rounds of golf at the Masters Golf Tournament in Augusta, Georgia. It is one of the great golf tournaments in the world.

A retreat for retired church workers is held annually in the Orlando area. This popular event, Veteran of the Cross, is attended by people from around the country. In 2008, Hu was selected by his peers to receive the Lloyd Behnken Medallion for faithful services.

One of the things we liked to do was to take groups on overseas trips. On one occasion we hosted 52 people (including 20 high school students) to the Holy Land, Jordan, Egypt, and Greece. A great spiritual experience we had was in the Garden of Gethsemane, Jerusalem, where we celebrated Holy Communion.

We rode camels from the hotel to the Great Cheops Pyramid in Cairo. A funny thing happened when we were climbing up the steep steps inside the pyramid. In the semi-darkness, a lady was coming down the steps and she called out, "Hi, Pastor Temme." She was a member of our former congregation in Centralia, Illinois. It's a small world...

A highlight of our trips to Jordan was the fortress stone city of Petra. References to this area are found in the Old Testament of the Bible. Petra once had an amphitheater carved in the rock which seated 8,000 people.

On three occasions we hosted tours to our homeland taking our American friends to Sydney, the Great Barrier Reef, Alice Springs and Ayers Rock (Uluru). These are fun trips to remember.

Each year on Chinese New Year, we gather together with our friends who retired from teaching in the Hong Kong International School. Many of them now live in the Florida area, and we dine in a local Chinese restaurant. Lots of memories shared.

A hobby of mine is to slow the extinction of the Monarch butterflies. We have milkweed (the butterflies favorite food) scattered around our garden. The butterflies lay their eggs on the milkweed, from the egg a caterpillar grows and then they make a chrysalis, and finally a beautiful butterfly emerges. It is wonderful to watch the progression of nature.

As a retirement gift, and returning to the states, our children arranged a balloon ride for us. We experienced the ride in Arkansas. We sometimes touched the tops of the trees, and other times dipped low down. It was an exhilarating experience as the silence was eerie. We could hear people of the ground below talking to each other. Then the silence was broken when the fire was turned on to raise the balloon over the electric wires, buildings and trees. People were waving when they saw us fly over.

We were flying high. And thank God, we still are!

A Note From Hubert

Congratulations my Dear. You finally did it!

Remember those happy hours at 5 pm when we had a glass of good Australian red wine to relax, to reminisce – and you said during our 20 plus years of busy retirement you must write our story for our children, grandchildren, and friends?

Congratulations my Dear – you did it. Not only are you a great typist but you are also a great storyteller with a fabulous memory.

Thank you for all you did for us Temmes. What a great cook, and frugal housekeeper living on a missionary salary. Those homemade clothes and knitted sweaters were very welcome.

But it is as a wife and pastor's wife that is your greatest gift to all of us. Just think about it – you attended every worship service I conducted – from the middle of the Australian desert to the historic church in Germany where Dr. Martin Luther was God's gift to the Protestant Reformation. How many pastor's wives can say that?

You accompanied me on so many home visits, made hospital visits yourself, prepared so many guest meals – and you were always a perfect hostess.

And what about all the different places to which God led us? When an opportunity came to move to another city or country your answer was, "Let's go!"

You picked a good theme for your book June. Truly God has Led and Blessed us far beyond our expectations. Happy Retirement.

Hubert.

Family Members

Joseph Graham (Joey) Temme born on October 2nd, 1995 in Hawaii.

Jessica Ann Schaub born on April 13, 1997 in Baltimore, Maryland

Jordan Elaine Temme born on January 15, 1998 in Austin, Texas

Luke David Schaub born on July 14, 1999 in Baltimore, Maryland

Our 10th and last grandchild, Abigail Leigh Schaub born January 7th, 2002 in Naperville, Illinois. All were baptized by their grandfather, Hubert Temme with water from the Jordan River in Israel.

Jill had major surgery, but recovered and Jill and Brad are busy enjoying their five grandchildren.

Lisa works for a Satellite company, and Greg for the Department of National Intelligence. They live in Leesburg, Virginia.

Our granddaughter Anne Temme, while attending the University of South Florida in Tampa, after leaving Stuttgart, Germany was stricken with Hodgkin's Lymphoma cancer and was treated for six months with chemotherapy. Five years later, our son Michael also had the same cancer. What are the odds? Praise the Lord, they are both cancer free.

Michael, promoted to Colonel, was the Commandant for three years at the Professional Education Center for the Army National Guard with 250 staff and 8,000 students in Little Rock, Arkansas. He served two terms of duty at the Pentagon and was sent to Bagdad, Iraq for 15 months where he was the liaison officer for the Coalition.

Our granddaughter Kristen Sprehe married Mark Kull in Louisville, Kentucky on 29th May 2010. Her grandfather, Hu Temme, performed the ceremony in a Lutheran Church. Our family attended this lovely event. They now have 3 boys, and 1 girl.

Grandson Kyle, married to Andrea, has one son, Landon, and lives at this time just 20 minutes from us. Granddaughter, Kristen Kull, lives with her husband Mark and their three boys, Waylon, Conway, and Calloway, and one girl, Gentry, living in Louisville, Kentucky. Kory is living and working in Tampa, and enjoying travelling.

Our grandson, Andrew, also in the Army, served a year in Afghanistan. We have a granddaughter, Jordan, and grandson, Luke, in Universities training for the Army.

Granddaughter Jessica, a senior in University, will graduate as a Pediatric Nurse. Joey is a University senior in Seattle. Abigail is a junior in high school and a great softball player and lives with her parents in Leesburg, Virginia.

Acknowledgements

My greatest fan for writing this book was my husband, Hubert. I am deeply grateful for the encouragement he has given me through this process.

I thank Barbara and Jim Bourland who directed me to a lady who helped me with my book.

Lil Barcaski - editor for the Ghost Publishing, who came to my house almost weekly to encourage and assure me I had a product that people would want to read.

To Eli Gonzalez of the Ghost Publishing who made it possible for me to publish my book.

Thanks to my good friends Anita and Dave Shrigley who told me years ago I should write a book. They were right, I should have written it years ago.

To Rev. David Paech, my childhood friend from my hometown. He and his family often visited us in Elizabeth, South Australia. We still keep in touch by emails.

To Val Dutschke, a college friend. We worked together with our husbands at Yalata Lutheran mission to the Australian Aborigines, and then they moved to the city of Elizabeth where my husband was the minister.

Rev. Dr. Dale Meyer, a supporter when we arrived in America. We were part of the same Lutheran circuit in

Southern Illinois, and have remained friends through the years.

To our many friends throughout the world who have stayed in touch with us through Christmas cards, phone calls, letters, emails, Face book, etc. You will never be forgotten.

About the Author

This book is the story of my life and family as a minster's wife. It has been a great life and this book, my labor of love is my legacy for my children and loved ones.

This is my story as I remember it. Finally, with the help and encouragement of my husband, family and friends, I have written this book for your enjoyment. I wrote it, not in my prime, but in my 80s. Being raised in a Christian home, attended Christian schools, married a Christian minister, and worshipped in Christian churches around the world, what could have been better!?

I guess God saw more in me than I saw in myself as He has led me all the way through trials and blessings. I have been married to a wonderful man for nearly 63 years. We have three children, ten grandchildren, and at this writing five great-grandchildren.

Thank you for reading the story of my life as God Led Me. Both Hu and I truly believe this because in all our ministries our joint theme was and still is Preach the Word and Love all the People. God's peace rest on all of you.

Blessings to all who read this book.

June